COMING TO COMPLETION

ii

I wish to thank the publishers, editors, and exhibiters who have helped my work come to the attention of the public. I also thank the many museums, libraries, and organizations that have supported the work of California writers of Native descent, and in particular, Heyday Books, Berkeley; the Porterville Historical Museum; Three Rivers Historical Museum; Tulare County Historical Museum; The Maidu Museum in Roseville; The Grace Hudson Museum, Ukiah; The Museum at Mickie Grove in Lodi; The Oakland Museum; Santa Clara University; and UC Irvine. I also especially thank Kaweah Chapter, Daughters of the American Revolution, and California's Eta Zeta Chapter, Delta Kappa Gamma, the Tribal Council of the Tule River Indian Reservation, Malcolm Margolin, for his long support of our state, its art and its Native Americans, and Lucille Lang Day's publishing house, Scarlett Tanager, for supporting poets.

COMING TO COMPLETION

NINE ESSAYS

On Simple Themes
personal and true

by

SYLVIA ROSS

Bentley Avenue Books

Books by the Author

Acts of Kindness, Acts of Contrition

East of the Great Valley

Ilsa Rohe ~ Parsing Vengeance

Acorns and Abalone

Lion Singer

Blue Jay Girl

Fables In An Old Style
Book One

Fables In An Old Style
Book Two

~~~<<<◊>>>~~~

This book is dedicated
to my good and long-time friends
although they already know
all its stories.

~~~<<<◊>>>~~~

Table of Contents

The essays in this book are mere vanities. They are observations from my life that, though true to memory, may be tainted by an eighty-year-old's sentimentality and rather outdated perspective. Though much of the essay, *Old Family Divorces*, can be documented, I only guarantee that the history passed on by my family's elders is as it was told to my sister Nancy and me years ago.

I wish to thank my friends: Sandra Arnold of New Canaan, Connecticut, for technical advice and editing, Bev Richardson, of Porterville, California, for her many years of friendship and excellent reading recommendations, Gloria Getman, of Exeter, California, for goading me into productive work, and Deloris Mahnke of Porterville, California, for so much good counsel — and her help on the most difficult day of my life, following my sister Nancy's death. I also thank Lanore Scott of Orange, California, Helen Lindstrom of Banning, California, Lois O'Connor of Camarillo, California, and Marilyn 'Winkie' Fordney of Agoura Hills, California for a *lifetime* of friendship, and each of the members of BOOKS, for their continuing friendship and support over the past quarter of a century.

✝ My husband proofed the book for me. We were amazed that our recollections — even to the long-ago words spoken — and quoted in the essay *Gravity*, were identical. Bob died on April 9, 2017, after the book's publication. In many ways, it is his book too.

sr / 1.25.2017

"Memory is a complicated thing,
a relative to truth, but not its twin."

Barbara Kingsolver
Animal Dreams

1942 ~ 1944

UNINTENDED LESSONS

UNINTENDED LESSONS

<<>>

I'm annoyed. My husband is driving to town for the third time today. For a man who unfailingly records every penny spent, he ought to consolidate all his errands into one to save gas and time. This is a recurring wifely complaint, but it is softly spoken. I do take exception to this habitual behavior of his, but my mother wasn't a woman who shouts. I'm not either.

I know our lives are for the most part shaped by lessons intentionally taught to us by our parents, childcare providers, family members, piano teachers, coaches, and the schools and churches we attended. We learned to be kind and fair, not to take things belonging to others, not to hurt anyone. The lessons we learned were designed to shape our moral values. And, if they were taught well, they do.

At the same time, other lessons were given to us. These, the *unintended lessons*, weren't so standardized as the *intended* lessons. They went wiggling around with variances from family to family. They weren't anything we were deliberately taught but were indirect, the result of our observations and experiences. Often, they had more impact on our lives than the lessons that were intentionally taught to us.

I realize I have to be fair. My husband's idiosyncratic travel urge is no more eccentric than my continual need to move furniture and repaint rooms that don't need painting. I know that he finds my impetus to disrupt the tranquility of our home aggravating, especially when he goes to sit down and finds his favorite chair in the wrong room. So, as his car goes down the hill on our bumpy dirt and gravel drive, my grimace turns into a smile. I send him a good wish, and hope he receives it. Is he looking in the rear-view mirror? Maybe.

My husband could go to town six times a day, and it wouldn't do me any harm. With his return from his travels, he cheerfully keeps me aware of buildings being remodeled, the efficiency of the new clerk in the Exeter supermarket, and what Caltrans is doing to the 198 and 65 intersection this week. Each return is a homecoming. Ulysses is back from his adventures; the sailor is home from the sea; the brave hunter is home from the forest.

I don't need to go anywhere. As a suburban child in the 1940s, I enjoyed a great deal of physical freedom. It is a good thing for children. With freedom comes practice in decision-making. That can make a difference in the choices we make as adults. It brought the kind of child I was the knowledge that I would lose that freedom if I didn't keep myself safe and out of trouble.

Every afternoon, when school let out, I was able to make a decision. Which would be the best way to go home that day? I could take the Red Car, or I could take the Metropolitan Bus Line, or I could walk.

The Red Car was so tall and high above the tracks I had to grab the bar beside the steps and pull myself up onto the first footing. It was exciting to climb aboard, find a seat, and wait for the rhythm to begin as the streetcar moved to clatter over the ties on the tracks. The seats were high and as plush as a throne. The Red Car was never as crowded as the bus, train passengers usually adults, bowed heads reading or knitting.

My mother preferred that I ride the bus, but it smelled of exhaust, and it was usually filled with noisy high school kids. The older kids were often snarky and rude to those of us in school uniforms, jibing about our religion. I preferred walking the three miles to West Side Village where I lived. I had carfare in my pocket. If I walked, I could stop at a store and buy gum or a candy bar. Or, I could save the money for Saturday.

On Saturdays, after chores were done, my sister Nancy and I went with our friends, Lanore and Leslie, to the Palms Theater to see the newsreels, coming attractions, "kiddie" serials, and cartoons.

On Sundays, after mass, if my sister and brother weren't sick with asthma, our family went to the beach, to a circus or carnival, or for a drive north to the San Fernando Valley or south to Knott's Berry Farm. At the very least, we had Sunday supper in a nice restaurant in Los Angeles. We children had plenty of entertainment. Even with wartime rationing, we often spent weekends up in Fresno with my mother's aunt Sade or down in Palm Springs or Lake Arrowhead with our Hungarian relatives.

However, my husband had a vastly different sort of childhood. He remembers being sequestered on remote small farms in Oregon and California for months at a time, to leave and return only by school bus.

Bob and his younger brother had cows to tend, apples to gather to feed the cows, rabbits to water, a barn to keep clean. There was little stimulation or entertainment other than the radio. In the brief period between homework and bed, the boys could listen. But with just one radio in the house, they didn't usually get to choose the programs.

Because of the work they were expected to do at home, they could never participate in any school sports or activities that went beyond three o'clock. The family's frequent moves to new properties and places between California and Oregon meant the boys were never in one school long enough to make any lasting friends.

Their family didn't join churches or social groups. The boys and their mother lived a seven-day-a-week work week that provided the labor important to their family's survival. They stayed home doing chores, while Bob's dad, a gregarious wheeler-dealer who made a living by buying, improving, and selling properties, came and went at will. The lesson that Bob learned, though not intentionally taught him, was that women and children were expected to stay confined on home ground. Men could come and go as they chose.

It was a grim, cheerless life. Bob talks of those isolated years very little, except to say that he was happiest when he was with his Grandmother Housdon. During the Los Angeles property acquisitions, he and his brother sometimes would stay with her on weekends. She had little money, but would save up to be able to treat them to the show or a bus ride to the beach.

His mother told me of the days during the Great Depression, and the years of World War II. She said that each day was like the day before, full of loneliness and dreary exhausting work. They didn't starve, but shampoo was a dreamed-for luxury. She washed her own and the boys' hair with Fels-Naptha laundry soap. The time when her children were young had been the worst part of her adult life. It should have been the best.

Yet, in spite of the extreme differences in our families, both sets of our parents worked hard to educate us to a common set of values. The values we were taught condensed to only one positive command: Be good. There was an unending list of negative values taught as commands: Don't steal. Don't lie. Don't hurt others... Today, while my husband wanders, and I work around the house, I ponder our differences from each other and think about all the many differences between the families we came from.

I look for whatever in them seemed so important that it could shape the idiosyncratic behaviors that cause us to annoy each other. We have value-driven behaviors that we share and other behaviors that we don't share — the former give us harmony — the latter cause aggravation.

The effects of the *intentional* education taught in our primary homes, classrooms, and churches shapes our moral sensitivity, and obedience to law, and they give us the skills we need in life. But the other kind of education, the kind that is *unintentionally* taught in that same childhood arena, directs many of our adult behaviors. That can dictate the many ways we may grow to be quirky, eccentric, or different from others.

I had much freedom to roam as a child, and as I ponder the reason why my husband continues to need reassurance that he is free to come and go. I also begin to study some of my own past behaviors.

As a young mother, I wouldn't leave my children with babysitters. I rarely ever left them even with their grandmothers. I trusted no one but my husband to keep our young sons safe. Until they began kindergarten, I was frantic with worry when physically separated from my children for even ten minutes. Somehow though, when a child reached kindergarten age, I began to feel I could trust the schools and the child's own wits to keep him safe. I no longer felt panic when he was away from me. But for the thirteen or so years that my husband and I had a child under school age, I was a rather crazy woman.

I was constantly checking my babies for fever, listening for every sniffle or cough, watching for any reduction in energy, examining every tiny scratch, getting up to check on them during the night, and sitting at a watchful window as they played in the yard. I overly worried about the possible illness of a neighborhood playmate giving *my* little toddlers germs. I'd even frantically wake them if they seemed to have napped overly long. I needed to confirm that they were only tired, not sick.

While Bob is away on his eternal cycle of easily deferrable errands, I think how amazingly patient that good man was with me during our early parenting years.

But why was I such an intense and fearful mother? Why would I never let a neighbor watch my little ones for even an hour? The neighbors certainly allowed me to watch theirs. Our house was usually full of preschoolers when any of ours were small. I was always home, a dependable neighborhood caregiver during those years.

Eventually the answer sneaks in between the broom and the dustpan. I was given an unintended lesson once. It was taught to me so long ago that I had forgotten if for decades. If I had ever flashed on a vague memory of that episode at all, I never thought to connect it to my compulsive, overly anxious, maternal quirkiness.

This is what occurred — and the answer I found. In 1941, I witnessed a serious accident that happened to my mother. Out of doors one evening, and heavily pregnant, she tripped over a garden hose. Calcium depleted from three pregnancies in four years, her tibia and fibula each were broken in two places and her ankle was crushed. She refused amputation. An orthopedic surgeon of renown was flown down from the Bay Area. He saved her leg but not as it was.

She was in the hospital for months while my sister and I were farmed out to relatives. When mother came home, our new baby brother and uniformed nurses came with her.

For a time, nurses in their crisply starched clothes and white shoes came to our house daily, but after they left, our mother still couldn't manage. She was on crutches and in much pain. We needed a full-time housekeeper, not just our usual once-a-week woman. However, the war had opened high paying jobs in the aircraft industry in our part of the city to women. Housekeepers weren't as easy to find as they had been before the war.

An older woman who had been trained as a practical

nurse before her marriage but now was a widow was recommended. She lived just two blocks away and could walk to our home every day. Our parents were grateful to find a woman with medical training, because although I was a healthy and rambunctious child, my two-year-old sister and our baby brother were both sick frequently.

The woman my parents hired, Mrs. Mourton, smoked cigarettes. Many of our mother's friends did. She had the common smoker's cough, as many of them did. Our parents didn't like the house to collect cigarette smell, but we lived in an area where windows could be open most of the time. However, she was clean, tidy, mature enough to be sensible, and she had medical experience. Her one flaw could be overlooked, and she was hired. Mrs. Mourton was conditioned from hospital work not to smoke constantly, and was given permission to go out on the patio when she felt she needed a cigarette break.

Our new housekeeper ran the household very well. Everything was soon in order, and my sister and brother seemed to be sick less often. I turned five and started to school. I remember that Mrs. Mourton was kind to us and on afternoons after school, she let me help her. I remember her kindness, especially since now I know what a bother I must have been to her. She worked for us for nearly two years, and then left her job in our home to move nearer her married daughter.

What followed was a series of housekeepers, some good and some bad. None stayed long enough that I remember their names. Either the work was too much, though our laundry was sent out and our mother liked to do the cooking, or they had a problem with the father of our family, a man who although he was generous, liked perfection and instant obedience. He showed his displeasure with far more drama than most American housekeepers could handle.

Mother grieved for Mrs. Mourton while I learned that small hands were capable enough to clean bathrooms and make beds. I could stand on a stool to scour the pots and pans and clean the sink boards. I could take out the garbage and care for my little sibs. I loved my mother, but our life was very difficult when the male head of our household was distressed, and after her accident, he was distressed very often.

One day in the spring when I was in second grade, a stern public health nurse visited us late one afternoon. I'd just come home. Our family was to be tested at a clinic.

Eavesdropping was my sister's and my favorite indoor sport. We paid attention when we saw the grim-faced woman with a briefcase come to the door. Though shooed away, Nancy and I crouched silently just around the corner of the hallway in a place where our floor heater vented from the living room and allowed sound to float down the hall. We heard what the nurse said.

Mrs. Mourton's cough was not from cigarettes. She had died. The nurse told mother that Mrs. Mourton's death was caused by long-standing, undiagnosed tuberculosis. Any family that she had worked for needed to be tested, particularly if they had children in the home.

Our mother's shocked responses rang out. "We aren't the kind of people who contract diseases." Then, "I would *never* have hired a sick person." Angry enough to raise her normally sweet voice, mother cried out, "*There is nothing wrong with my children!*" Nancy and I silently listened.

The nurse insisted that everyone in the family be taken to the doctor, and we were forwarded to a clinic where x-rays were made of our chests. Although Mother persisted in saying the government tests were wrong, it was proved that although our parents' and my lungs were clear, and we tested positive only for exposure, my siblings' X-rays showed an indication of small, healed tubercular lesions. We were not sick or contagious, but the government had not been wrong. Mother never spoke of that again, and I think she carried shame from the incident — something she couldn't possibly have helped — for the rest of her life.

Our parents investigated, and they found the best children's doctor available in Southern California, a Beverly Hills pediatrician, Dr. Ezra Fish, who had been chief of staff at Children's Hospital. We never developed active T.B. Nancy and Joe's asthma was carefully monitored. From that time on, the children were able to be active and miss school less often.

My stepfather, who I then believed to be my father, had a brother who, with his family, visited us frequently during the time Mrs. Mourton worked in our home. Tragically, our uncle and cousin contracted the disease. Our cousin eventually made a good recovery. But our very loved uncle, who had kept us happy in heavily accented English by telling us Hungarian jokes, stories, and songs, died of tuberculosis in Oliveview Sanatorium in 1946.

From that early exposure to TB, I would show a false positive on a tuberculin tine test, and would be later required

24

as a teacher in the public system, to have a periodic chest x-ray, while my unexposed co-workers only needed to take the simple blood test. I still ask Dr. Bruce, our beloved long-time internist, for chest x-rays. Symptom-less, I still fear I might put a grandchild — or great grandchild — or any child at risk. My lungs always pass. His eyes twinkle, and I'm sure he thinks I expose myself to radiation more often than necessary, but he deals with my anxieties with ever-patient kindness. He knows my concerns aren't totally without justification. At least to me.

I've finished cleaning the kitchen and bedroom. I ought to be thinking about getting supper organized. There is still time to plan a dessert for the two of us. I have all the ingredients I need. I'm smiling to think that I won't have to send Bob back out to get sugar and eggs. Not that he'd mind.

I keep dawdling, going back to the effects of the unintended lessons. Of course, by the time I was in second grade I already knew very well that children could catch illnesses from other people. After all, my little sibs caught chicken pox from me, after I caught it from a schoolmate. People caught colds from other people. And since the vaccines hadn't been developed, they also caught chicken pox, measles, scarlet fever, and mumps.

But the subtle, sneaky way we were exposed to tuberculosis, the way the common cigarette cough in those days camouflaged that disease, and the shock of the mandated visit of the public health nurse to our home, put an umbrella of anxiety over me.

That umbrella wasn't apparent during my school years, but would come back and shadow me when I was a woman with children. As I'd *intentionally* been taught not to steal or cheat or lie, I'd been *unintentionally* taught what can happen to a family. Years later, I wouldn't be comfortable putting *my* babies in anyone else's care. I trusted my husband, and my children's grandparents. I didn't trust anyone else.

How patient Bob was during that time. In my over-reaction to a childhood lesson, I felt an overpowering mistrust concerning caregivers for our children. That eccentricity changed the way we lived our lives. My husband and I were to spend fifteen years scarcely ever going to a restaurant, or movie, or taking a weekend away from our children. We didn't socialize. If I needed to go to the doctor or some other place, Bob arranged his schedule to be home with the boys or I took them along. He attended the conferences at school for our older children so I wouldn't have to leave the younger.

I've always tossed attribution for those fifteen years of isolation from parties, dinners, shows and concerts to not having enough money. The truth is that staying home had little to do with money. Bob would have much enjoyed dancing or going to a show. But not accompanied by a nervous, jittery wife who wanted to return to her babies ten minutes after having arrived. Going places or not going places was to insure my comfort. He stayed home with me, accepting the way I was, and he never railed at me or accused me of being odd.

I'm an old woman now, and he is an old man. It has taken me a very long time to recognize the effects of Mrs. Mourton's unintended lesson and appreciate the value of having a spouse who had the patience to deal with years of what might be seen as abnormal, agoraphobic, and annoying wifely behavior.

Enjoy your trip to town, sweet man! I won't complain anymore about your restlessness. Go as often as you like.
Bring me tales of whatever you see. Every one of your homecomings fills me with joy.

~0~

The Persistence Of Memory

THE COLLECTED
JACK LONDON

THIRTY-SIX STORIES
FOUR COMPLETE NOVELS
A MEMOIR

Ivy Housdon Ross 1912 - 1992

THE PERSISTENCE OF MEMORY

<<>>

I write. It is a compulsion as much as an art. If no one ever read what I wrote, I'd still be at the keyboard, as happy as a stone-age petroglyph artist drawing in a cave.

Today, I was reworking a presentation I must soon give for a writer's group, but I paused, distracted by thoughts of my mother-in-law. It is her birthday. She has been dead for twenty-five years yet I still miss her. And although my mind is jammed with my own memories, I know how good our minds are at stealing other people's memories. I must confess to stealing — and using — one of hers.

An artist, popular in the mid-twentieth century, expressed the way memories slip through time in a well-known painting familiar to most of us. The painting is called *The Persistence of Memory*. It is by Salvador Dali, and it hangs in the Museum of Modern Art in Manhattan. In it, as my eye beholds the painting, time and memory seem to blend liquidly into the present and slide into the future. A fond remembrance compels me to stop my work and spend time thinking of Bob's mother, and of the way I used her memory.

My mother-in-law was born on December 4th, 1912 in Holiday, Texas. Four years later, something very harsh happened to her. It didn't cause physical injury, but the horror of it was to persist in her mind throughout her life, and quietly take up space in mine. Long after she was dead, the incident she shared with me surfaced as I was writing a novel.

I was nineteen when I met Ivy in 1956. She was my boyfriend's mother. We were to be friends until she died. Ivy was a small woman, a natural blond with blue eyes. She used few cosmetics and wore simple clothing. My first impression of her was physical. She was very pretty, and had a great smile. Her teeth were nice, not so common in the days before children commonly wore braces. Cigarettes had aged her skin a little, as it had some of my girlfriends' mothers, but Ivy was still as slim as a girl, and as quick and agile. My second impression was rather more thoughtful. The keenly observant social reserve that had first attracted me to Bob had come to him as a genetic gift from his mother, along with his fair, handsome features.

Bob's parents married very young, and they struggled through dire poverty during the depression. But they were wiry, energetic, and determined. Their life together was built of hard work, frugality, and predictable habits.

Cigarettes, coffee, and the use of a few minor vulgar words were their only vices. They owned a modest house on the border of the communities of Lawndale and Manhattan Beach. Prior to that time, they had lived on successive rural and semi-rural properties, in and out of California and Oregon, improving them, selling at a profit. It had been a hard life, and Ivy was determined she would never move again in her lifetime.

Bob's father had been born in the Polish ghetto of Milwaukee in 1909. He had taken a stepfather's surname as a boy, hence the name Ross. But Bob Sr. was similar in his style to others of his Polish lineage, the actors Paul Muni and Charles Bronson. He and Ivy were a good match. He was no taller than I, but was muscular, and aggressive. Bob Sr.'s size didn't keep him from being tough. Bob's mother had been born on a ranch in West Texas. She was from old American stock. Four of her ancestors fought in the Revolution. Ivy and Bob Sr. met in Long Beach, California in 1929 when he was stationed there in the navy. They married when he was twenty and she just seventeen. He had dropped out of school after seventh grade. She hadn't finished high school.

My mother-in-law led a rather solitary life and was comfortable with it. As a stay-at-home wife, she had never learned to drive. This was not uncommon with women of her generation. In Los Angeles, in the fifties, dairies', bakeries', and ice cream vendor's trucks came down neighborhood streets. Pharmacies, laundries, and some liquor stores still delivered. Many homemakers didn't drive.

Ivy kept busy with the laundry on Monday morning, ironing and mending on Tuesday, making a cake from scratch on Wednesday, and so on through the week. Her time, day to week to month, was plotted ritually and seldom varied. It matched the embroidered 'day of the week' tea towels one sees in antique shops today. She had a cat she was very fond of to keep her company. While the Ross home was small, and though not what one would describe as especially stylish, it was about the cleanest house I'd ever been in. The ashtrays were promptly emptied, and everything that needed putting away was put away. In the evenings, she crocheted while tolerating her husband's choices on TV. She told me once that anytime a show came on the screen that she thought she might enjoy, he changed the channel.

She took this kind of mild bullying as a small price to pay for having a loyal, non-drinking husband who was home with her every evening. Too, she was proud that *she* had never had to go out and work for wages "like some women have to do."

Usually, on Saturday nights, Bob's dad took Ivy to Hawthorne, a neighboring town in Los Angeles, where they met their friends and danced the one-step. Often friends, more her husband's than hers, met with them during the week to play pinochle or Yahtzee. She liked playing cards, but they never played for money.

She was at her happiest babysitting Bob's niece, her little granddaughter Jacquelin, and when analyzing difficult crocheting patterns and working in her flower garden.

She was pleasant and likeable, but her nature wasn't social, and she was happy with her routine. It would never occur to Ivy to do anything so frivolous as go shopping with neighbor women, or spend money out on a lunch with the women who were part of Bob Sr.'s and her circle.

Bob's father was the more sociable of the two, but he found jovial daily contacts with people through work was as much human contact as he needed. He had retired to live on the income from his property investments, but he did his own maintenance of the properties he owned. He had many manual skills and would do odd jobs for friends. Even though he liked to brag that he could afford not to work, he enjoyed the camaraderie of other people he found when working.

34

Casual camaraderie would stay at the job sites. Bob Sr. would never do anything so financially frivolous as step into a café or go into a bar without his wife. They both were very circumspect in their behavior. Ivy would have faced doom rather than be thought a flirt.

I'd had had a very different parental modeling. Now a widow, my mother was plump, sociable, and self-indulgent. She had suffered through tragic losses in her life, but they had never been economic losses. My mother had been a 'fought over' child, the subject of custody battles, and had been married a number of times. By her mid-forties, she'd survived the deaths of two husbands. With my stepfather's death, she had determined that although she had lost her husband, she would never be 'a poor person', or have to go to work.

Although she had a good income insured from her business properties, she expected my sister Nancy, brother Joe, and me to cover all our own expenses and contribute money to the family. It was fair to charge me. I was nineteen and working full-time. But my sister and brother were still in in high school. Our mother, who had never been poor was irrationally afraid of poverty, though she had never had to worry where her next meal would come from, nor had she ever had to wear second-hand clothing as Bob's family had.

It was more that she liked comfort and nice things. She certainly didn't want to lose the freedom that she had always enjoyed or any of her comforts.

My mother enjoyed cooking, having her hair and nails done, party going, and shopping. Household tasks weren't her forte. Sewing made her nervous. Ironing gave her a headache. She would fit into today's culture much better than she fit into the domestic culture of the 1940s and '50s.

My friends' mothers were proud of their homemaking skills. They knitted and sewed. To describe my mother's lack of domestic industry to my friends I'd say, "When our hems came down, my mother took my sister and me to the Broadway for new dresses." Sometimes we went to Bullocks in Westwood, but usually the Broadway Crenshaw. Occasionally mother let us stay home from school to go shopping and out to lunch with her. My sister and I loved the department store tearooms, as did our mother.

At the time I met Ivy, the woman who would become my mother-in-law had probably never been inside a posh Department Store. She was very rarely in a grocery store. Her husband did the shopping. Once every month or two, Bob Sr. would take her to Woolworth's to buy yarn, sewing needs, or a lipstick.

A couple of times a year Bob Sr. would take Ivy to J.C. Penny's for her clothing needs. Every three weeks she went to the barbershop with him and the barber trimmed Ivy's dense curls in a boy-cut. Any manicures she had, she gave herself.

Ivy and I liked each other from the first. Our commonality had little to do with the way we looked. We were physically different. She was different from her daughter-in-law, Patricia, also. Bob's brother Pat's wife had a good relationship with Ivy just as I did. Ivy was very fond of us. We two were dark while Ivy was fair, but our values were very similar.

The woman who would become my mother-in-law was a woman of strong convictions, and she rigidly held what is now called "a moral compass." She was absolutely honest. That was culturally different from the "never say what you think, always say something nice" conventions — and pretensions — of the nineteen fifties I struggled with.

My mother had tried hard but failed to instill those "nice lady" conventions in me. They seemed dishonest, and I wasn't good at decoding that what I was told was always what was meant when something nice was said.

With Ivy I felt as comfortable as I did with my girlfriends. I could say what I thought to her as I did to them. If she disagreed, she said so. She might be wrong, but she would never lie. There was nothing duplicitous or manipulative about her. And she didn't expect other people to hold her same opinion.

Bob and I became engaged. Since our homes were a great distance from each other's, we'd spend weekends alternately staying with either my family or his. At his house, while Bob put in long afternoons studying, I would spend my time in the kitchen with Ivy. I soon realized that I could be very happy living her kind of life. I too liked solitude, pets, a garden, a clean house, and needlework. Her life was predictable. I liked that. We spent hours at the kitchen table on those quiet afternoons, as she crocheted or mended and told me of her life. I liked listening to her memories.

A hundred years have now passed since a grim incident happened to Ivy, the episode that was to work its way into the novel I was writing. It never left her mind, and flowed as a liquid into mine. As I was in the process of writing *East of The Great Valley*, the incident almost typed itself into the novel's manuscript. This is the true story that Ivy told me:

The scene opens in the barn of a large ranch in Texas. It is a bright day in the spring, of 1917. The characters are J.B. Miller, a grain farmer in his late sixties, his four-year-old granddaughter Ivy, and a kitten. They are in the barn. The child is playing with a litter of kittens. Her grandfather tells her she can play with them, but not to take them outside.

He says he doesn't want them in his way out by the wagons. They should stay with their mama.

He goes out to repair a wagon's axel, and Ivy picks a playful black and white kitten as her favorite, puts him in her lap. She lets him climb on her shoulder and chew at her hair. After a time, the she has to use the outhouse. She doesn't want to leave the kitten. It has fallen asleep in her lap.

But she needs to use the outhouse and doesn't want to wet her pants. So she gets up and goes outside into the sunshine, carrying the kitten with her. Her grandfather, tinkering with the axle, growls at her. He reminds her what he said.

She goes back into the barn and pretends to put the kitten down, but smuggles it under her sweater. She is enjoying the sensation of its tiny sharp claws clinging to the yarn and pricking at her skin as she sneaks past her grandfather.

In the outhouse, she puts the kitten on the bench of the two-seater and struggles to get her sweater off by herself. In the struggle, she bumps the kitten with her elbow. Its little claws can't get traction, and the kitten falls down into the pit. The child lets out a wail and wets herself. She starts to sob.

Her grandfather rushes to her. He's alarmed, until he hears the kitten's hollow mewling and assesses what has happened.
He scolds the girl and pushes her back up against the planks of the outhouse wall and tells her to "stay put." She is too frightened to move — frightened the black and white kitten will die, and frightened she will get a paddling.

He leaves her to fetch a narrow, wooden ladder and bring it back. He lifts the two-seater's bench on its hinges and puts the ladder down into the filthy sludge at the pit's base. Then, he takes off the child's shoes, stockings, and sweater. He swings her onto the ladder placing her feet on a rung just below the opening.   He orders the child to go down into the dark, fetid muck at the bottom, saying, "You put him down there. You get him out."

She cries and blubbers, but he blocks her way and won't scramble up and off the ladder.

Afraid of the big, stern man, she works her way down into the stink and reaches for the filthy kitten. Then, holding the slimy kitten in one hand, and with only the other to help her climb, she stumbles back up to the top. Her grandfather takes the kitten by its neck and then helps her off the ladder with his other hand.

They go across the yard to the pump. He roughly washes them and the kitten clean. She is barefooted and her clothes are wet but he makes her take the kitten back to the barn. He says, "Remember, girl. You're responsible for what you do."

I knew how I could pluck out fragment from Ivy's story and make it fit into the grim scene in my manuscript, and knew she'd not mind that I used it.

Later that same year, 1917, Ivy's father found that he could make more money in the oilfields of California than laboring on his father-in-law's ranch. My mother-in-law grew up in Southern California. The rest of her life, Ivy had a cat, and no desire to return to Texas.

My mother-in-law would have recognized that my use of a memory she had given me was a way that I brought her back to me. I could never forget it, or her.

This story, Ivy's memory, was not the only shadow crossing the novel's pages as I wrote. After I recognized the origin of the section I was writing, I began to feel that there was another outside source that was contributing to the novel I was writing. It bothered me. I know nothing is original. Everyone in the arts borrows from the whole of their experience and it is filled with all we have seen, heard and read. Worried that I may have unconsciously plagiarized another writer, something I am scrupulous never to do, I mentioned my fear to my husband.

I outlined an episode in the novel that was troubling me. Bob first suggested William Falkner's work might be a possible influence on the scene I'd created. I shook my head, knowing the source would not be Faulkner. Then he suggested Jack London's books.

That author seemed right. I hadn't read Jack London for years, maybe not since college. I gave Bob a kiss for the idea and went straight to the bookshelves. He was right. London's story that had left such an impact on my mind is called *Samuel.* It is from Jack London's book, published in 1914, titled ***The Strength of the Strong***.

The point of derivation in Jack London's story affecting mine was too vague for it to be a concern for my work or me. The character in London's work is more pathetic than evil.

The episode in *East of The Great Valley* where I introduced him is far different from the story *Samuel*. But how long the persona had lingered in my memory that so many years later it would come and be an influence on my work! Do we ever truly forget anything?

I gave my evil character a name to reference Jack London's character in *Samuel*. London's rugged work is not as popular or as frequently read as it once was. I doubt that he is an assigned author in today's high schools. But, maybe some reader of my book, who feels the same fondness for literary masters of earlier times that I do, will feel the shadow — and go to his or her bookshelf for a re-read of *The Strength of the Strong*.

~0~

LOVE, UNDER THE SIGN OF CANCER

<<>>

My sister Theresa is the hero of this story. She's attractive, droll, and always entertaining. She keeps me either grinning at some incident in her shop or rolling my eyes at her adventures — like canoeing through caves in Belize. My mother's last child, Theresa is much younger than I. She is intense, but slips easier into a smile than a frown. She is a person who people notice and remember, while I'm the kind of person people forget as soon as the introduction ends.

Though we had the same mother, my sister and I are not like her. We each take after our fathers in our looks and personalities. They were very different types of men. Theresa's father, who had been an immigrant from Hungary, was a magnetic, friendly, energetic and successful retail businessman. He liked proving that America's streets were indeed paved with gold. At one time, he owned three liquor businesses in West L.A. Her father liked fine dining in good restaurants, dressing well, and showing generosity to others.

In opposition, my father, the descendant of taciturn Scots, was an introspective craftsman who spent his vacations in the Oregon woods. He had been a chief mechanic and engine design implementer for both the North American Aviation and the Douglas in Santa Monica, California during his working life. He liked flying and earned his 'wings'. He liked building furniture and playing cards. He had two friends, Bill May, an administrator at Sawtelle Veteran's Hospital, and George Brent, an actor. For him, the company from two good friends and one wife was all the sociability needed.

I was nearly sixteen when Theresa was born. When I was married, she was my four-year-old flower-girl. Another sister and two brothers filled the gap between us. A single important thing that my sister and I share in common is that neither of us knew the fathers we are very much like.

I'm so timid that an old cousin of our mother's once snarked, "That Sylvia is so scared she wouldn't ask for a drink of water if she were dying of thirst." Theresa, my opposite, is gregarious, independent, and bold. She power-walks two miles each morning through the desert and up through Sedona's red rocks. She manages a grand home, a demanding husband, busy family, and a time-consuming business. She is a master at 'how to get things done' and skilled at on-line research. She knows where and how to get the best deals on everything from vehicles to sports socks. My sister wouldn't be intimidated by anything. If she were suddenly through some magic appointed Chief Justice or Attorney General of the whole United States. She likes to fight for truth. She'd get busy and research the job, learn the skills she needs, and get to work.

Theresa's birth was a great joke the stars and planets played on our mother. Mama had converted to Catholicism a few years after she married my sibs' father. Then some years later, when she had a very demanding husband and four children already, at a time when birth control was largely ineffective, our mother found herself pregnant for a fifth time. She was forty-four. My stepfather was sixty-two.

She had never planned to have children. But she could not bring herself to have an abortion, and she was married to a man who took pride in the children she gave him. Now close to menopause, she was tired of dealing with asthma, measles and chicken pox. She was tired of having to shop for children's clothing and shoes, and birthday party gifts, and new tires for bicycles, and deal with lunch pails and broken thermoses, and laundry in those pre-clothes dryer days. She was in her mid-forties, and ready to find for time for herself.

As much as my sister Nancy and I tried to help, Mama told the two of us that she thought her life had come to chaos.

48

With no escape possible from this late life pregnancy, our mother spent time in church lighting candles and attending novenas. Because she had confided in us, Nan and I knew she was dropping coins in the poor box in hopes God would grant that this last child would be a girl. Mama didn't like boys very much. She prayed for a tranquil, no-trouble girl.

Mama trusted that God in his mercy would answer her prayers and give her a daughter. She refused to even consider boy's names. She said the energy and noise boys brought into a household wore her out. Our brothers were good boys, Joe was thoughtful and John was full of fun. Neither was any trouble to her. But her mind was set against their gender. I liked our brothers and their friends. I remember telling Mama I was going to have six boys when I grew up and got married. But I didn't cheer her up or change her mind.

Our mother chose to name the coming baby after St. Therese of Liseaux, Mama's favorite saint. Therese of Lisieux was a reticent nineteenth century saint who spent her adult life as a silent, cloistered nun. Our mother felt that this would insure that this baby would reflect the saint's peaceful, prayerful nature. Mama didn't anticipate that God might think she was being greedy. And Mama forgot there were <u>two</u> Saint Theresas.

Obviously from the way our sister turned out, God favored St. Therese of Avila over St. Theresa of Lisieux. Unlike sweet, simpering St. Therese of Lisieux, St. Therese of Avila was a fearless activist. She was a nun with the moxie to set the church on its head with her demands way back in the sixteenth century. And right from the cradle, our baby sister was bold in her demands. She had the right name, but it came from the wrong saint. At least Theresa was named for a saint. Mother named Nancy and me after her favorite movie stars.

There had been a grave downside, pardon the pun, to mother's choice of husbands. Our plump, soft-voiced mother was attracted to older men who were financially secure. As our fathers were older husbands, they were more likely to die sooner than younger husbands might. That happened. My father died of pancreatic cancer before I was a month old. Theresa's and my other sibs' father died of emphysema and heart problems the day after Theresa's second birthday.

Unfortunately, our mother had been an only child and her parents were dead. Raised to be sweet and pretty, and having little or no work experience, or inclination, Mama was left with no one to help her deal with a thriving retail liquor business, rental properties, and five children aged from two to seventeen.

It was a very hard time for her. But she managed and didn't take to drink or pills. The upside was that Mother's gentle, languid appearance hid the fact that she actually was a strong and tough woman, as all the women in her family before her had been. She survived as they had survived by being decisive and never giving in. Our mother's survival mode was the place where Theresa was raised.

We older children were seldom around, and we had been raised in a different kind of family than Theresa was. There had been a man during our early years, a man who spoiled our mother and indulged the family. He wasn't there for Theresa. She watched as her mother coped, and grew aware of how to use the strength a woman can summon when she needs it.

My sister also, was to become a single parent. And when that happened, she knew how to do whatever had to be done to raise her child and support herself.

After my sister left her first husband, knowing she was clever and capable, she managed well. She'd always been able to find a job even as a kid, and knew neither she nor her child would ever starve as long as she could work. Attractive and personable, but concerned for her daughter, Theresa did well.

She briefly pursued acting. Living literally between two film studios, she had the contacts and opportunities many women dream about. Theresa had a few appearances on a TV soap called *The Days of Our Lives* and hoped for a spot on a more popular soap, *The Young and The Restless*.

But as a single mother, worried about her child, Theresa needed steadier work. She decided to enroll in beauty school. She liked art and it was an art craft. She was confident that as a stylist she would have job security. Even in hard times, women want their *color* and the luxury of feeling well groomed. The profession also offered flexible work hours. She would be able to work and still get to school conferences, pediatrician appointments, and manage days when school was out.

Theresa made a good decision. Naturally, Mama didn't mind occasionally babysitting a granddaughter, but only occasionally. Theresa could raise her daughter well on her own. Eventually, my sister remarried. Her second husband was nice looking and good to her and her daughter. Everything seemed going well, until one day my phone rang. Mama, sounding very concerned, called me one evening to tell me, "Your baby sister has done a terrible thing! She has left poor Jim and run off with some man from Arizona!"

In spite of our Mama's own history with multiple husbands, she was scandalized that my sister would leave a perfectly adequate husband. In Theresa's defense, I pointed that out. But Mama remained judgmental, making a point I had heard many times before. "But I was a poor motherless child. I didn't have a *mother* to teach me to do better. You three girls did. I *raised* you to know better."

Our mother's dismay turned out to be short-lived. It only lasted until she actually met Theresa's "man from Arizona." Then Mama was as charmed as if Theresa's new man were a combination of mom's all-time favorites, Gregory Peck and Omar Sharif. I'd never heard her talk so glowingly about a man ever! And it turned out that we sibs and our spouses, were as charmed as Mama was. When we met Bill, we all liked him. He was an early retiree, clever, artistic, and tolerant. Bill owned a grand multi-layered home he had designed and built on a hillside in Sedona and welcomed all our families.

Our sister was surely, purely in love. However, no matter the situation, Theresa looks out for the future. Before she left her secure job as a colorist in a nice salon, she had to be guaranteed an income of her own.

She had practical, good sense. She wasn't a woman who wanted to be dependent on *anyone* other than herself. She never had been, and liked the independence. Bill helped her open a salon in his town. It was successful. She knew she would do well and she did. The population in that beautiful area, old and young, male and female, locals and tourists, all wanted expertly colored hair.

The windows of Bill and Theresa's house overlook the red rocks of one of the most beautiful places on the planet. When she goes to the market or to do an inventory in the salon, Theresa may wear sweats and a runner's headband, but anyone can see that the diamonds on her fingers are real. My sister and Bill have had a lovely daughter together, and Theresa's older daughter from her first marriage and her family live in Arizona now. My sister's life is almost perfect.

However, almost perfect isn't the same as perfect. Though you wouldn't notice it because of her vitality, my sister is a stage-four lung cancer victim. And, she has had two other unrelated cancers. Theresa's father was health-conscious and though she didn't see him being careful in diet and exercise, she is his child. She has taken good care of her body. My sister has never smoked cigarettes or anything stronger.

In addition, she has no familial history of cancer through either of her parents. My sister isn't without faith. Although she isn't the kind of Catholic who goes to mass every morning or makes a novena whenever she twists an ankle or scubs a toe during her morning trail walk, she is an oddly spiritual person. Not that it's odd to be spiritual, but it's odd for someone who is so active and so aware of the real world. Always looking for something more, she reads self-help books and the books written by what used to be called 'faith healers'. I respect that, although I don't quite understand what she expects to learn.

Long before she had cancer, Theresa told me about an author whose philosophy and spirituality she admired. I knew I'd inherited my taste for fictional literature from the father I had never known. But Theresa evidently inherited her taste in books from Mama. Though she shuns reading the novels I love, and hasn't read all of the ones I've written, my sister owns *every single book* written by a man named Joel Osteen. The only book I ever remember our mother reading was **The Power of Positive Thinking** by Norman Vincent Peale. It fits.

Several years ago, Theresa's disease led her to very good thoracic oncologists. A later metastasis in an eye led her back to Texas and the ocular oncologists at M.D. Anderson in Houston. Those marvelous doctors have kept her not only alive, but vigorous. People meeting her for the first time would never guess she was a stage four-lung cancer patient. So, when one of her quarterly PET scans showed new reason for alarm, a mass on a kidney, there was only one thing to do. She and Bill got in the car and sped to Houston.

As an outpatient at M.D. Anderson, having been examined, Theresa and her husband had to wait over a weekend for biopsy results that would better define this new kidney cancer and set its course of treatment. They grew bored in their hotel room and decided to tour the Johnson Space Center hoping for distraction from the waiting ordeal. Houston is not Las Vegas or South Beach, Miami, but it has its attractions. One of them is the Space Center. The Center has daily visitors from all over the world. My sister and Bill both enjoyed reliving their memories of the era of America's astronauts and "Houston Control," and capturing the excitement they felt when man first walked on the moon.

They stayed in the building until it was closing time, and the docents were ushering visitors out. The danger of cancer held at bay that afternoon by their awesome reminder of the wonders of the universe beyond our little planet.

Afterward, instead of driving back to their hotel suite, my brother-in-law had an idea he was sure would make my sister happy. He asked Theresa if she'd like him to drive her by the church where her favorite author, Joel Osteen, preaches. He had a map of Houston's high points and knew he could find it.

If, like me, you don't follow celebrities, Joel Osteen is a kind of positive-thinking celebrity-preacher on TV. Bill is a skeptic like me. But he loves my sister. He knows reading Osteen's books makes her feel empowered and good about life. I don't understand her fascination as well as Bill does. My sister has lived her life as though she has *always been* empowered. She is a very decisive person. I couldn't see that she needed any more empowerment than she already had. But then, I'm not the one with cancer. It is Theresa who keeps me informed about who's who in movie and TV celebrities in this century. She has spent so much time in doctors' offices and hospital waiting rooms scanning People Magazine and Sports Illustrated, she knows who everyone is. I've never seen this Joel person. I watch TV, but not that kind of TV. I'm more a Law and Order re-runs, PBS, or STARZ channel watcher.

In spite of the unfamiliar horrendously busy, late afternoon traffic in Houston, my brother-in-law easily found

Osteen's venue. Theresa got her iPhone out so she could take a picture of the Houston mega-church as they drove by. There was a yellow-painted curb parking spot being vacated just across from the church's main door.

Bill swerved their car into the spot. He told Theresa to hurry but hop out and get her picture of the entrance. He didn't want to get a ticket. She got out and ran across the drive to ask the attendant at the church entrance about the legality of parking in the yellow. The attendant gave her an "all okay" sign and laughingly teased that in Texas yellow paint on a curb meant, "first come, first served." He then invited her to bring her husband into Lakewood Church and enjoy touring around. I know all these details of their day because we are sisters, and our phones reach easily from Texas to California.

While they wandered around the edifice, the choir was practicing and Music surrounded Bill and Theresa as they spent most of an hour on their informal tour. Then, as they left the building, the attendant invited them to come back in an hour, assuring them that Joel Osteen was in town and Osteen was scheduled to preach the evening service.

There was a restaurant down the street. Theresa and Bill were both feeling invigorated and ravenous. They hadn't thought about food all the while that they'd been at the Space Center or wandering through the huge church. During their supper, Theresa chattered on about Osteen's philosophy and more than once thanked Bill for his thoughtfulness in suggesting that they visit the church. She felt she had been to the shrine of a man who, if he wasn't one of the hallowed saints of her Catholic school childhood, was certainly one of her adulthood's heroes. She wanted to go back to the church that evening, and was chattering to Bill about the possibility.

A couple eating nearby, hearing her happy exclamations, turned and introduced themselves. They explained that they served as ushers at Lakewood, and they warmly invited my sister and her husband to meet Joel that evening. They promised to get seats for Theresa and Bill right down in the front at the service.

The couple kept their promise. That evening, Theresa and Bill met and had their picture taken with the famous man. They met Osteen's wife and mother also, since both were celebrants with him at the Houston church that evening. Joel Osteen and his family very graciously took time to chat with my sister and my brother-in-law, asking them first where they were from, and then why they'd come to Texas. When Osteen learned that Theresa was in Houston as a cancer patient at M.D. Anderson, he showed great concern.

He asked her if she would like him to perform a 'healing' for her. My sister was beyond thrilled; for a moment, she was breathless.

Even so, she wasn't speechless. Theresa thinks quickly. As I told you, she is bold and forthright. She knows what she wants. She spoke directly and turned down her hero's heartfelt offer. It wasn't because she was a Catholic, and Osteen was another variety of Christian. It was because her odd spirituality kicked in. She wanted the healing done, but she didn't want it done by the famed preacher. My sister, politely and sincerely, told Joel Osteen she hoped he wouldn't mind, but *if* it were all right with him, she would rather have the healing done by his mother.

The celebrity preacher most gallantly and graciously gave his approval. That evening, Joel Osteen's mother, Dodie Osteen, performed a healing ceremony for my sister. My sister found it a powerful and deeply moving experience.

Theresa returned to the hotel with Bill that night, and felt rid of her medical anxieties. A few days later, after she had undergone more tests, the biopsy confirmed that this was a cancer, but one unrelated to her original lung cancer and not a metastasis. This was actually good news.

A continuation of her primary lung cancer in the kidney would have been more immediately dangerous to her life. Theresa stayed calm stayed calm and felt serene. She called to tell me all that had happened. After assuring me that although she would be having surgery on the kidney, she told me she knew that everything was going to be all right.

When Theresa recounted the event at Lakewood Church to me, I know she anticipated that my agnostic non-believer's eyes would be rolling. But they weren't. I love her and had been very worried about what she would learn from the oncologists on this fourth-time cancer had found her. I wanted to believe that the healing would make a difference. But, I know how bold she is, and I was shocked at what she had asked of Joel Osteen. "I hope you didn't hurt his feelings," I said. As I said those words, I could hear our mother's voice and intonation coming out of my mouth. I started to apologize, but she interrupted me.

"Well, I can't be bothered by anyone's feelings right now," Theresa snapped. "His mother is a *woman* and I know that's where his power comes from! That's where Joel got his, straight from his mother. And you know I needed the most powerful, *very best* healing I could get."

Theresa called me this morning. The kidney surgery wound has been long healed. She had just climbed the trail to the top of Sunrise Mountain to greet the sun, as she tries to do every day. She had funny stories to tell me about her shop, her neighbors, and Bill's latest fixer-upper classic car. She'd passed her last scan and was happy. I may still be a skeptic. But my sister is still alive.

~0~

nb. *In 1959, a nuclear disaster occurred at the Rocketdyne plant in Simi Valley. It was kept secret by the government. News of this accident did not appear in the papers, nor was it mentioned on radio or TV. Our family home in Granada Hills, California was 14 miles downwind from the accident.*

We older children had married or gone to jobs. But our younger brother John and sister Theresa were still kids, swimming in the pool and riding their bikes all around the neighborhood. Both those two younger sibs have had multiple cancers. There is no cancer history in their family on either side. We older sibs are free of cancer as of today.

For information about the nuclear accident, go to:
www.nbclosangeles.com/investigations/LA-**Nuclear**-Secret-327896591.html or do a general search by typing in: nuclear disaster Simi Valley.

The Significance of a Story's Title

~~~<<<◊>>>~~~

ABOUT A STORY'S TITLE

<<>>

Yes. *If* you are an avid reader, you noticed. The title on the essay about my sister, ***Love Under The Sign of Cancer***, is very similar to the title of a very famous novel written by an internationally known, Nobel Prize winning, twentieth century novelist. Gabriel Garcia Marquez's great novel, ***Love in The Time of Cholera*** is still in print and still praised.

In case you have suspicions that this *almost* title theft of mine from another author's important book might not be ethical, relax. This isn't considered plagiarism. Titles don't fall under copyright or intellectual property laws. I am very fond of Marquez' book, and could legally have called my story ***Love in The Time of Cholera*** if I'd wanted.

I didn't. My sister has not had cholera, and titles shouldn't mislead. My intent was only to give a humble nod to one of my favorite writers, an "Honored Sir, Good Author, I salute you," and not to steal his words. Should any of you still be concerned, here is how it works with titles: They can't be stolen, because they can't be owned.

A poem of mine was used in a rather elegant anthology a few years ago. It was put together by a couple of professors at Sierra College in a tribute to authors who wrote of the Sierra in California. The title of the anthology was *The Illuminated Landscape*.

It featured writings about the Sierra by not only contemporary writers, but also by a wide range of writers from earlier days. My little poem is in its pages, keeping company with work by Isabelle Allende and Mark Twain, Jack Keroac, T.C. Boyle and Wallace Stegner and others. On its publication, I had been sent the usual contributor's copy, but when I went to amazon.com to order a copy to give as a gift, I found that there was more than one book with its title. I had to enter the subtitle to find and purchase the book I wanted. I needed to type in *The Illuminated Landscape*, *A Sierra Anthology*. Adding either its subtitle — or listing the editors' names — along with the title was necessary to obtain the right book.

Often an author will use another author's title unknowingly. I seriously doubt that when the talented Canadian poet Gil Adamson chose *The Outlander* as the title of her novel, she even knew that Diana Gabaldon had written a series of books with the exact same title. I didn't. I'd read Gil Adamson's novel. It was years later that I first learned of Gabaldon's books when some friends mentioned a TV series of that title.

Often, a title or reference to a title is used as an act of homage. I'd read Gabriel Garcia Marquez's book back in the late eighties or early nineties. It is one of my great all-time favorites. And. when I was writing about my sister and her struggles and the moment of feeling victory over her disease, a reader familiar with his writing would recognize why I'd chosen to imitate the rhythm and tone of Marquez's title.

I admit to being a constant, but shallow reader. I see and understand the socio-political implications of complex novels. But they aren't what I remember, not what I take away from the reading. I remember simpler human things. *Love in The Time of Cholera* was an important book and a beautiful one. But what I most remember is this:

The book tells of a long relationship between two people. They meet when young and they want to be together, but life and circumstance separate them. The woman marries someone else. Some years later, the man again sees the woman with her husband at a public event. She has borne children and now seems dumpy and old, while her dapper, elegant husband is in his prime and more attractive than when he was younger. It is a sad observation the man who had loved her makes in the book, the observer feels disillusionment that the woman he loved is no longer at all what she was.

Years later, far into the storyline, the man has an occasion to see the couple again. The years have changed the woman's elegant husband into a withered and fragile, hunched old man. While the woman, also twenty years older now than when he saw her last, seems unchanged from what she had been at mid-life.

That perception carried so much impact for me that I still remember it. I remember it clearly, though it has been many years since I read the novel that I can't remember the names of the characters in the book or the twists of the story's plot. *Love in The Time of Cholera* made me look around at people I've known throughout my life and understand that achievement is no more to be prized than endurance. And that observation is somehow appropriate to my sister's story. Theresa endures. She has achieved also, but endurance means she doesn't wither under what life brings, good or bad.

The themes that writers use won't fall under copyright law either. Another important book carries the almost identical humanist theme that Gabriel Garcia Marquez's book does. It is a book by an internationally notable author writing during roughly the same time period as Marquez.

Again, I don't recall the grand exercise in history and political presentation that the similarly themed book gave its readers, nor can I recall any examples of its author's use of the *magical realism* as a literary device that made his books critically noteworthy. I read the book very long ago and my memory is feeble.

I only remember a simple, very human episode, a single paragraph from a book of hundreds of pages whose author became a celebrity by alienating his religious leaders. The book I read is *Midnight's Children* by Salman Rushdie.

This isn't Rushdie's more notorious book that called down an Islamic 'fatwa' condemning him. This is one of his other books that my friend Bev recommended, after my limited brain and its even more limited imagination caused me to bog down in the fantastical chapters while I tried to read Rushdie's much discussed *The Satanic Verses*.

My friend was right. I liked *Midnight's Children* very much. (Thank you, Beverly. I have always been able to trust your recommendations.)

Midnight's Children compelled me to deal with elements of fantasy and magical realism that are beyond me as a reader. I'm comfortable in a realist's world, either sordid or sweet.

Rushdie's novel took the *Man Booker International Prize* for its excellence in displaying the tensions of a nation moving from colonialism to full autonomy, but all my limitations of memory allow me to remember today is a vividly humorous, human scene. Here following is a summary:

An old grandmother is forced to move with her large family far from their homeland. They must move far from their homeland. She copes with the change, but doesn't want to be cooped up in the huge multi-family household. She wants to own a petrol station. And she sets about building one. As it is being erected, she oversees the work, goading the workmen into working harder and better. She recognizes that her body's circumference has increased since she was young and beautiful, and she knows that her girth will probably continue to grow. She urges the men she has hired to build the little cash-cubby where she will sit selling the petrol to make it wider and wider until she is satisfied that it will accommodate her eventual size.

It is no wonder that although I've forgotten most of the plot, I haven't forgotten that old woman.

Rushdie's **Midnight's Children** is very like Gabriel Garcia Marquez's **Love in The Time of Cholera**. Both books bring the reader to the enormous capacity for endurance of women, a value stronger and longer lasting than achievement.

My sister Theresa isn't a novel reader. But she was our mother's last child. She, who was still home with our mother as the rest of us moved away, knew mother best. Theresa trips along believing in things spiritual and knows how to survive the difficulties of life. She didn't need to read Marquez or Rushdie's books to recognize and understand the fundamental enduring power of women. Theresa learned it by her earliest childhood's observation.

~0~

On Being A Poet

ON BEING A POET

<<>>

I've been a reasonably successful minor, regional poet. I've had poems published in magazines, and my work has been included in a number of anthologies. *Acorns and Abalone*, a collection of poetic work and drawings, has sold well — considering it is a book of poetry. And in 1988, I won a money prize in the only poetry contest I ever bothered to enter. Not much money, but I bought a Stetson hat with it. It seemed appropriate that a poetry prize go to my head.

Publishers of school texts here and in Canada have asked permission to use my work, and beside the poems, I've published three novels and four children's books. While not widely known or advertised, the books have earned me a bit of spending money. At least on a regional level, I've been recognized for my practice of the art of writing. But I've made very little money on the poems. It isn't a commercial art. Poetry is the kind of art one practices only if one's living comes from somewhere else.

Our art is filled with our lives and experiences. My family lived in a lot of places that I still remember, but never in a real suburban type of neighborhood until 1942, when I was five and old enough for school. We'd lived in apartments where the neighbors were all adults or in the living quarters of our stores. Customers to liquor stores in that era weren't children. Until school, I'd rarely been with children my age, though I had a baby sister and brother. I had second cousins, Ann and Jane Fenton. But they were some years older than I, and we didn't see them often. The age difference made me see them as adults, just more interesting than most adults.

When I reached five, my parents bought a real house in a real neighborhood with a lawn and back yard. I started first grade against my will. I was too afraid of the other kids to talk even at recess. Children were foreign to me. Most had turned six already and were larger than I. I thought I'd been thrown to barbarians. (And yes, I'd heard the term and had a general idea of its meaning.) I hated the circle games the sisters encouraged us to play, and for nearly a year until I mastered the language and natural belligerence of children, I just wanted to go home and be with my mother, small sister, and baby brother.

I spoke to no one in school. Not talking had some advantages. The sisters liked children who were quiet. I never was pinched or poked with a pointer by the woman in the veil and long black dress, though I saw that noisy and rude children often were.

I could read a little before I started school, words my mother taught me from storefronts and street signs and the labels on bottles in our stores. School gave me the *sounds* of the letters as we read about **Dick and Jane** and filled in the blanks in Think and Do books. By Christmas I was reading well. Though I still couldn't figure out which way to run in the circle games. Which way was left? Which was right?

Sister Viator read stories of the saints to us every morning after the pictures on the Bible charts were explained and prayers memorized. The stories were of the visitations of angels to earth and of miraculous happenings of the saints. I liked the stories.

My second-grade teacher, Sister Theresa Josephine, suggested that my mother take me to the library because I'd read all the books on the classroom's free-reading shelf. That didn't work out. My mother, a semi-invalid at that time, didn't like having to drive me there and back or to pay late fees. But our cousins' mother kindly drove over from Glendale and brought a big box of her daughters' out-grown books to our house for me. The box, filled with classics written by Frances Hodgson Burnette, Enid Bagnold, Louisa Mae Alcott, Carolyn Keen, and P.L.Travers became my sister Nancy's and my treasure chest. I'm ever grateful to my mother's first cousin, Viola Roscoe Fenton.

Before St. Augustine's School, I'd never heard anyone read aloud, other than on the radio. My mother read magazines. But she read silently, not to us. The man I thought was my father read *Magarság*, a Hungarian newspaper, along with the *Los Angeles Times* and *Herald Express*, but he too read silently, not to the little ones or to me.

Reading was something grown-ups did, and my progress turned me free. In fourth grade, Sister Stanislaus told the class that one of the requirements for sainthood was proof of 'bilocation of the body' and that saints like St. Francis had been proven to be in two places at once. I wanted to believe in saints and miracles but I'd learned to be suspicious of what adults said. Still, with a book, I could bi-locate my mind. I could see there were others in class with a storybook hidden below the desktop. We knew to bring our attention back to the front of the room if Sister was saying something important about latitude and longitude, or fractions. Later, I'd realize Sister Stanislaus was giving silent approval to our furtive activity, reading 'on the sly.' That love of reading would lead to our writing assignment proficiencies and would carry over into other subjects.

In spite of an unfortunate tendency toward occasionally using phonetic spelling, I earned the English Award at the eighth grade graduation of my school. Our Irish-born nuns who taught at St. Augustine's and St. Paul the Apostle School in Westwood were so demanding, that I'm more proud of the eighth grade award than I am of a much later earned college summa. Following St. Augustine's School, at the Catholic girl's high school I attended, I began to write verses that that the editors of the school paper liked. My poems were trite bits of artsy religious fluff with predictable rhyme and meter. I was writing the kind of stuff that one finds in church bulletins and children's magazines, and in the big print publications that one sees in waiting rooms and doctors' offices.

The nuns who taught in my high school were dedicated. They gave us reading lists and encouragement to learn. The school library supplied me with books. I began to identify what I most liked.

As I read, I found that the verse that I was writing wasn't the kind that I liked. I was vain and enjoyed the attention school publication brought me, but I took no pride in what I'd written. I had come to appreciate poets whose work was vastly beyond my ability. I'd learned to discriminate and was now shamed and embarrassed by every stanza I'd ever composed.

The commercially popular poets of my student days were Ogden Nash and Dorothy Parker. Their writing seemed almost too smug in its cleverness, cartoonish, and doomed to be short-lived. Humor's impact died after the reader smiled. I acknowledged those clever poems; saw how they escaped being doggerel. However, they didn't linger in my thoughts. My admiration grew for Robert Lowell's war laments, the poems of Archibald MacLeish, Wallace Stevens (*Thirteen Ways of Looking at a Blackbird* - a lifetime favorite), I loved Robert Frost's work, Edna St. Vincent Millay's verse too. Though my teachers didn't find Millay work so praiseworthy, I so liked a poem of hers I'd read first in 1952, that riding the Staten Island ferry was more important to me than seeing the Empire State Building or Trade Towers when I visited New York twenty-five years later. I wanted to feel what Millay felt that inspired *Recuerdo*.

The early nineteen-fifties were too early in time for Zora Neale Hurston or Maya Angelou to be taught in high school, but Langston Hughes's verse prodded my sensitivity to the girls in my classes who came from other Los Angeles neighborhoods, not the all-white west side. Poets' phrases repeated in my mind. Their rhythms sang to me in Mozart or Bach's cadences and in the music of Olvera Street or jazz or Hungarian violins. It was the music of my city, and it was verbal music and not what I'd been writing at all.

It wasn't in the nursery-rhyme meters of the churchy verse I had been writing. I admired those writers too much perhaps, because when I was sixteen and entering my senior year in high school, I stopped writing. I refused to provide any more verses for holy cards, pamphlets, or the school newspaper. I was disgusted with what I had produced, embarrassed by the folly I'd written and then had seen look back at me from print. I knew that I would never have the intellectual insight or the nimble vocabulary necessary to write like the poets I admired. Shamed, I abandoned the one area where I'd been singled out for any kind of praise. My poetic career was over.

Nearly a decade later, as a woman expecting my third child, and taking a class at Fresno City College, I began to write again. I'd made some simple rules that allowed me to indulge in the poetic scribbling I'd liked to do when younger:
1) I wouldn't show my work to anyone else.
2) I wouldn't compare my work to the work of others.
3) I wouldn't write anything shallow, obvious, or slick.
4) I wouldn't compromise for a readership

Compromise led to glib verse, the vanity of my girlhood. (Eventually, I would break the rules. But I tried to keep them.) Fortunately, when I went to FSU in the late sixties, I was able to study with fine teachers in the college. Phil Levine was on staff at FSU but on sabbatical when I was studying there. But an already acclaimed poet, Robert Mezey had taken his place. Bob was a gifted teacher as well as a poet. He taught us three important things. The first was simple: Avoid abstract nouns. Truth and Beauty might have value, but they have no common meaning. A poet must use concrete terms with universal application to be fair to his or her readers. Bob Mezey's second lesson was more difficult. A poet must explore all the darkness in his or her own experience as thoroughly as he examines the light. He taught us that only by bringing our own shames, humiliations, and guilts to our consciousness, to balance the triumphs our pride and vanity never let us forget, would we develop the insight to have a true poetic voice.

His final, epilogue demand seemed silly. He insisted that any original work we presented was to be signed, dated, and show a copyright symbol or notice. It seemed a joke to most of us in his classes. None felt that our work would ever be read by anyone but a very few friends and fellow students. Who would want to steal it? Mezey's rule was proven valid. A student in another writing class was expelled from the university for submitting another student's work for publication. Our naïvely intense group of student writers was appalled. What worth had stolen art to an artist? None at all.

I was also fortunate to be in classes with others who became recognized poets. Dennis Saleh, Omar Salinas and Greg Pape and I were FSU's students chosen to represent our school at UC Irvine's Manuscript Day for Poets in 1969. We, with representatives from other California universities, were feted for a weekend, and our work was published in a small journal celebrating the event. Four decades later, I was pleased to be again a guest at U.C. Irvine, and read my work there once again.

I've been invited to give readings in many venues and colleges. Four must be an auspicious number because four poets from the anthology, **The Dirt Is Red Here,** *(2002, ed. Margaret Dubin, Heyday Books, Berkeley, CA.)* were invited to read at the International Modern Language Association's Conference in San Diego in 2003, as in 1969, I was one of them. My poems are few. They often take years to complete. I've completed no more than fifty. I've practiced the art with limited fluency. It is a serious flaw that I regret. One fine and talented poet I know has published at least nine chapbooks. Another, no less talented, has boxes of unpublished work never even submitted. However, slow though I am to finish a poem, I have never abandoned the art again. I still keep lines on scraps of paper, waiting for the right words to work out a satisfactory bit of verse that paints a particular thought that I can't convey in prose.

I appreciate that I've had the opportunity to know other poets, literary artists whose work I greatly admire. Some of them have been recognized and have had fame. Others have not. But we all share a dedication to our chosen craft.

Practicing this particular art has given a grace to my life. And it has brought an honest pride when the work that meets my standards is recognized, and a bit of joy when the doggerel I write (as on the back cover of this book) makes someone smile, even if it won't stay in the reader's mind long.

I studied fiction writing also, and have done well, regionally. Still, once, back in the late sixties, Allen Ginsberg visited Fresno State. On the second day, following a hugely grand campus "be-in", Ginsberg gave a reading of local and student work to crowd of writers. The group had gathered at a ranch Bob Mezey and his wife rented out in the hills east of campus. Following his reading of some of my poems, Ginsberg said of my work, "This poet has a voice."

Poetry is my favorite art. I'm grateful to the teachers who taught me where to find a voice, and how to use it.

~0~

GRAVITY

A LOVE STORY

GRAVITY
- A Love Story -

<<>>

Choosing a mate is a grave and serious activity. Only a most frivolous or desperate person would latch on to another person and assume happiness ever after. I have always been a grave and serious person and was conditioned by my childhood to be extremely wary of men. So, I was more careful than most.

Dating and early marriage was both expected and encouraged in the mid-twentieth century. These were the days before pregnancy could be avoided as it can now. The cultural ethic for middle-class Americans was that early marriage was preferable to botched abortions and over-crowded orphanages. Teenagers were thrust together and expected to pair up. I lived in a city where it was normal for high schools to have over a thousand students. Colleges and Universities were large also. There were many jobs that put young men and women in easy proximity. That gave a girl plenty of choices before she reached her late twenties when the gong "It's never going to happen" began to strike.

I began dating in 1951 when I was fourteen. By 1954, I was so disillusioned that I contemplated a single woman's life.

By 1956, I was determined I would lead one. I didn't mind becoming an old maid sort of woman. That didn't seem all that terrible, though most of my friends thought it the worst possible thing that could happen to a woman. I had a job I liked, and could imagine sharing an apartment with other girls from the ink and paint department, or better yet, renting an apartment on my own and getting a cat for company. As far as sex went, I knew I could live without it. I'd not yet tried it, and didn't think I'd missed much.

But the snag was, I wanted children someday. I was very jealous of my mother. I loved my younger brothers and sisters and felt she hadn't appreciated them enough. I wanted children of my own, more than two. I'd read that donor sperm were now being used to inseminate women whose husbands were infertile. The process was called artificial insemination. The Pope had come out condemning its use. But while my mother was very religious, and horrified by the idea, I wasn't. It sounded like a marvelous idea to me.

So I set a goal. By the time I was twenty-five, I'd either have found a man I liked enough to consider having sex, or I would move to a part of Los Angeles where I could bear and raise scientific-bastard-children without causing embarrassment to my mother.

This was a logical and reasoned plan. I'd never have to live with the torture of pretending to love a man that I only liked, and no man would be around to treat my children badly. I gave up accepting dates at all — except with a few men I'd met through church singles clubs' activities in the city that had become friends. They took me to dinner, shows and club dances and made no demands other than friendship. By hindsight, those nice men were probably as frightened of the physical expectations of dating as I was, some of them probably closeted gays. But in the fifties, everyone was expected to date in gender opposing pairs, and no single girl went out on a Saturday evening without an escort.

But then, in late August of 1956, I met Bob.

Some of my friends and I were in our usual Friday evening-after-work pub, sitting at a long table. It was crowded, and I was uncomfortable. Two tall, hulking and brash guys were hanging over me trying to get me to talk to them. But I didn't know them. They weren't from the adult church group I was with, a C.Y.O. singles 18 - 35 club from my home parish. I didn't recognize them as part of Ridley's usual Friday night college kid crowd. The men were too close. They were bothering me. I tried ignoring them, but it only seemed to make them more persistent. Men had always frightened me, particularly large men. I'd dated frequently, but only with men I'd met through school friends, or the church group, men who were polite and well recommended. I'd avoided men who were aggressive or rude.

Lois, my friend, had driven us to meet our group that evening. She made me promise we would stay until at least ten. She was talking with a guy I knew she liked. I was shrinking down, not looking at either of the hulks. They took that as encouragement. I wasn't playing coy. I just wanted them to go away and leave me alone, but was too frightened from childhood experiences to lash out at anyone, and certainly not at two men who were so big.

Though busy talking to Ryan, Lois was watching. She saw my discomfort and whispered, "There is a guy over by the bar who looks very nice. He's been watching you ever since we came in tonight. If you smile in that direction, maybe he'll come over and scare those guys away for you." Lois was always giving me advice I didn't particularly want, but we'd been friends since fourth grade and she noticed what was going on better than I. So, I glanced toward the bar but saw only a shadowy blur of shapes.

The brutes were still trying to get me to talk to them.

I wanted to go hide in the ladies' room, but they hemmed me in. I couldn't get out without pushing past them. I tucked my head down. In less than a minute I heard a calm and clear male voice saying, "Go on, you guys. Give the girl a break." I looked up to see a slim, nice looking blond man confront the hulks. He'd pushed in between the table edge and their bodies. Though they were taller and heavier than he, the hulks moved back. One of them made a mocking bow, and then the two laughing, jiving, and staggering over each other, retreated. They blurred into the crowd singing at the piano, their broad backs to the tables. I felt free again. I could breathe.

The man who had sent them away looked down at me and smiled. "They are really good guys. They wouldn't have hurt you. They just drank a little too much tonight." His smile was shy and understanding. He stepped back. He *didn't* move in on me. I hesitated, not saying anything to him. I just nodded. He smiled, then I did. Lois and Ryan—the guy from our C.Y.O. group that she was interested in—had been watching. She nudged me and winked. This was the man at the bar.

Lois gave Ryan a look. He'd been sitting directly across from us, and he slid farther down the bench. I wasn't sure I wanted the man to join us. But when he looked down at me questioningly, it seemed as though he'd only sit with us *if* I wanted him to. I gave a little nod of approval.

The man who saved me wasn't one of the glib college kids in Ridley's. But he wasn't *old*. Lois and Ryan began talking to him. They explained that our group was from a young singles club from a church in Culver City, and they asked him about himself. I listened and found that his name was Bob Ross. No, he wasn't a Catholic. Yes, he was a full-time student at USC. Yes, that's where he'd heard about Ridley's. Yes, he had a job. He worked thirty hours a week at a place called H. I. Thompson.

He seemed older than the giddy college kids hugging the piano. I thought he might have been in Korea and spoke up to ask, "Are you on the G.I. Bill?

He turned slightly away from Lois and Ryan to look at me. "Yes," he said. He didn't turn back to them.

"What branch of the service were you in?" I asked. I allowed myself to make eye contact.

Bob shrugged, made a little grimace, and said, "Oh I served my time in the Coward's Navy." Then seeing that I was confused by the term "Coward's Navy, he clarified the phrase for me. "I was in the Coast Guard."

My rescuer grinned a little. "It was a way to keep from killing Koreans, or having them kill me."

The humble candor of this man endeared him to me. I thought that it seemed natural that a Coast Guardsman who was used to rescuing people would rescue me. But I didn't say any of that out loud. I merely said, "I think you made a good choice."   We began talking, and Lois and Ryan's attention went back to the club members farther down the long table.

I had grown so tired of the swagger, strut, and verbal braggadocio of the boys I'd dated in high school and the men I'd dated after I'd gone to work, that this man was refreshing. Besides, it just seemed sensible to me that someone would choose a way NOT to go to war. My shyness disappeared.

I noticed that the man had clear summer-reddened skin, blond streaks in his light brown hair, and blue eyes with pale lashes and brows. He was fair, but had a five-o'clock-shadow on his jaw. I found that attractive. The singing grew louder at the piano. "Pack up all my care and woe, here I go singing low…" My friends were still all around us, but the man who had saved me and I closed them, and everyone else, out. This man was soft-spoken, but he was knowledgeable and could actually talk about more than sports or politics.

Bob said that he'd been unusually lucky in his service-time. He'd been stationed in Santa Barbara for a year and a half, then in New Orleans to finish out his term of duty, when he could have been sent to Adak or Greenland. In New Orleans, he had been infected with the sounds of that city's classic old-style jazz at Preservation Hall and bars in the quarter. His face showed his enthusiasm for the rowdy music of 1920s-30s, a parallel genre to the old songs we sang in Ridleys.

I told him that I worked for Disney in Burbank, where the members of the Firehouse Five band worked, and that when they were getting ready for a gig, they'd get together up on the third floor of the animation building to practice. I was often able to spend my lunch hour with other girls from the ink and paint department listening to them practice.

Although I'd danced at the Aragon Ballroom to Lawrence Welk's band, and I'd danced at the Palladium to Billy May, Stan Kenton and others, I was enthusiastic about the band I knew best. No music was as lively or as *danceable* as the Firehouse Five's beat. We grinned at each other finding we had a fondness for the same kind of music. I felt a little dishonest and confessed that I'd been into classical music all through school, and it was still my great favorite listening when I was at home or as I drove to and from work.

He said, "KFAC. Yes, me too!"

Bob knew who Mozart was, and how his music differed from Bach's. It turned out he also knew who Bruegel was, and how that painter differed from Jackson Pollack in more than just centuries. He didn't care for Dos Passos's writing but he enjoyed Steinbeck's. He told me that he grew up reading Nordoff and Hall. Those books from boyhood prompted him to be a reader. That prompted him to go back to school after the service.

That night at Ridley's, I found that Bob was a delightfully grave and serious person. This kind of man would never think that taking a woman on a date entitled him to spout out a pompous, patronizing *"what I like in a woman"* speech. More than once I'd demanded that a date take me home before we got to where we were headed because there was no point going further. No matter what exciting venue we were scheduled to attend, the date was over. I would never ever make myself over into some man's idea of what I ought to be.

This man, sitting across the table from me right now, spoke to me as if I were another *person*, not just another ponytail with big boobs. We talked on until it was well past ten and Lois was elbowing me, telling me it was time to go.

If it wasn't love at first sight, that Friday night in Ridley's, it was definitely love at first conversation.

That August, neither of us missed showing up in Ridley's on Wednesday and Friday evenings, traditional 'stag nights', finding each other and talking. I had some dates tentatively scheduled for club activities on Saturday nights, but hoped Bob would ask me out, and he did. He invited me to a party the office staff at H. I. Thompson, where he worked, was having on September 30th. I gave him my address and phone number. He promised he'd call to firm up the time.

It was a nice party. Bob's co-workers seemed to like him. We left after a couple of hours. I declined stopping at a drive-in. There had been food at the party. But he seemed reluctant to end the evening, and I was reluctant to go home. He stopped at a small bar out near the airport where he knew there was live music. It was dark and smoky, but we found a table. He ordered a beer. I asked the waitress for bourbon and tap water. This place didn't have the raucous banter of Ridley's. People weren't singing around the upright piano harmonizing to *Shine on Harvest Moon* or *Bye, Bye, Blackbird*. It had a small dance floor. We danced more than we talked that night, and I got the rather nice sensation that my body liked him as well as my mind did. That was a new kind of scary.

As he was driving me home, we talked about music, my work at Disney, his office job, and his classes at the university. We were in conversational harmony until after a few moments of silence, he said, "I didn't know you drank."

I took it as criticism and became haughty. I snipped back, "Does that bother you?"

"No. Why would it bother *me*? I was only a little surprised because I've never seen you drink anything but Seven-up at Ridley's."

"Well, I can't drink there. We don't want Ridley's closed down for the violation. Where would the Sinners and Saint's club go on Friday night?"

He frowned, and asked, "How old are you?"

"Nineteen." I answered.

Bob stopped for a red light. As it turned green, he stated, "I don't date women under twenty-one." He seemed offended, as though I should have had my age stamped on my forehead when we met. I would have told him, but in all our conversations at Ridley's, age had never come up.

Now I was offended. "How old are *you*?" I asked him. "I don't date guys *younger* than twenty-three. Men usually outgrow being stupid by then."

He said, "I'm twenty-five."

He was watching traffic and didn't see me smirk. Sarcastically I said, "Well, you've passed *my* criteria."

Without either of us saying much more, Bob turned the car onto my street and drove up the hill, parking in front of my family's house. He opened the car door for me and walked me to the house's front door, nicely thanked me for the evening, and stood on the porch until I was safely inside. It was well past midnight. My mother, sisters, and brothers were asleep. I got ready for bed quietly, thinking that Bob was as grave and serious as I was and probably wouldn't want to date me again. I liked him, but I'd understand. Before I fell asleep, I decided not to go to Ridley's the next week, no matter how much Patty pestered me to go with her. Bob would either call, or he would not. I didn't want my physical presence to goad him into doing something he might not want to do.

He called on Tuesday evening.

Age, the first hurdle in our relationship, had been jumped. We were together every weekend after that call. I could get tickets to Disneyland, and he took me to *Aida* at the Shrine Auditorium, and to listen to Dave Brubeck at the Lighthouse in Hermosa. One Saturday evening at a venue down in Los Angeles with some studio friends of mine, Bob met Ward Kimball, Jimmy McDonald, Frank Thomas, and others in the Firehouse Five Plus Two, the band whose members I knew from work.

Distance became the next hurdle in our relationship. As weeks progressed, that second hurdle in our relationship was already growing worse. Bob already had to travel a long way to see me. We had each come to Ridley's, which was near the intersection of La Brea and Jefferson, with different groups and from far apart neighborhoods. Bob lived miles southwest of the airport, on the border of the towns of Manhattan Beach and Lawndale. I lived miles to the north of LAX on the border of Palms and Mar Vista.

The distance wasn't so great if one could drive through air, but the hills and sea cliffs of western Los Angeles determined the configuration of streets and roads.

As if the distance weren't already difficult, my widowed mother sold our west side home. She found tenants for her business properties and had purchased a new house being that was being built in very far Granada Hills. The new house my mother liked so well would be ready before Christmas. After we moved, I'd have an easier drive to work, but it would be almost impossible for Bob and me to continue seeing each other.

Very few freeways had been completed by the mid-fifties. The Hollywood and the Pasadena Freeways were still new, work on the Harbor Freeway had been begun but would take years to complete. There were none yet through West Los Angeles. This meant that Bob would have to drive a minimum of an hour and a half, most of it on Sepulveda Boulevard, the old Highway 99, to get to Granada Hills.

The best route for him to take would be from his home in Lawndale via Imperial Boulevard to Sepulveda Boulevard (Highway 99) past LAX, down Baldwin Hills, across the Culver City-Westwood plain and up through the twists of the Santa Monica Mountains.

Once across the mountains, he'd have to cross the San Fernando Valley. In traffic, this could take well over two hours. The general Los Angeles area is very large.

I was sure this would end our relationship and dreaded having to say goodbye to this man. I really liked him. As it turned out, the strength of our attraction won over both my regrettable youthfulness *and* the Southern California distances. Bob made the long commute.

Our parents would be the third hurdle that presented itself. My mother, though she didn't like little boys usually did like men. But she wouldn't accept my choice. She couldn't understand why I had turned away from all the men I'd dated that she'd liked, only to settle on the one man she didn't like.

She complained often. "Your Bob is nice looking, but he isn't friendly." Or she'd say, "He's so austere and standoffish." She warned me that I'd never have any fun if I married a man like Bob. Mama hadn't noticed that I wasn't a person who cared much about what she called 'fun.'

He certainly wasn't standoffish with me, and I loved the safety I felt with this scholarly, thoughtful man's arms around me. After my mother met Bob's parents at their home, she took exception to the neighborhood where they lived.

It wasn't a bad neighborhood, but the lots weren't as wide as ours, the houses not as uniform in style. She wasn't happy.

My mother bluntly told me she wasn't happy I was dating a 'working class man' from a 'working class' family.

Then I upset her when I answered that I thought *we were* working class people. I pointed out that none of her children were encouraged to go to college. We'd been encouraged to go to work. Nancy was in her senior year of high school and working almost full time in retail. My brother Joe, only a junior, was also working nearly full-time after school and weekends. John, just a little kid, was talking his way into a caddying job at Knollwood Country Club well before he was old enough to be hired. We seemed like working class to me. Other men I'd dated may have worked in insurance agencies or in white-collar jobs, but they weren't doctors or lawyers.

My mother liked Bob's father. She said he was a little crude, but then added, "Oh, but your Bob's father is so energetic and witty, He's a lot of fun." She added that she thought Bob's dad looked like John Garfield, one of her favorite movie actors.

There was some conflict points with Bob's family too, although they seemed to like me. Bob's father wasn't shy about saying what he thought.

Although he was charming with my mother on the rare occasions they were together, and in spite of her liking him, Bob's father didn't quite approve of my mother. He said that he thought her "hoity-toity," and complained to me during the preparations for our wedding, "Your mother sure likes to put on the dog." I smiled at a trace of hidden joke in his slang. My mother preferred silver fox. But, I knew what he meant. She fussed about things that weren't too important.

Shortly before our marriage, Mama reiterated her objections, saying: "Another thing, Sylvia, that you should think about. Pay attention to what I say. If you marry him, you'll have to watch yourself carefully. He's the kind of man who has absolutely no spirit of forgiveness. Everything is black and white to him." I think what I liked most about him was that he was so principled. He did see things in black and white, right and wrong, but I did too. Besides, I didn't plan to ever do anything that would require forgiveness.

One day, I pestered Bob to tell me his parents' reaction to our planned marriage. He reassured me that his mother liked and approved of me. I'd felt that she did. But I wasn't so sure of his dad. I'd overheard his blunt talk about my mother, and rightly assumed he would have had some criticisms of me also.

"And your father?" I asked, "What does he say about me?"

Bob frowned, shook his head, and said in his honest way, "You don't want to know."

"Yes, I do. And I won't get my feelings hurt."

He gave me a quizzical look. "Really?"

I said, "Yes, really. I'm not hurtable by just words."

"Okay, if you honestly want truth, here is exactly what my dad said. "'Well, Bobby, she's a goddamn Catholic! You'll have a houseful of smelly, squalling brats by the time you've been married five years. I know she has a great figure, but God Damn, son! You ought to know that by the time she's forty, those tits'll be down to her knees.'"

We were married June 15, 1957. I wouldn't need artificial insemination to get the children I wanted. Lois was one of my bridesmaids, and the same hulking brutes who had been annoying me at Ridley's in August were sober, tuxedoed ushers at our wedding.

Bob's dad thought his son was making a big mistake, but he was willing to be present at the ceremony — provided my mother didn't expect him to wear a "God Damn tuxedo!" As soon as we were free to live where we wanted, we moved far enough to prevent his father and my mother from complicating our lives, but stayed close enough to visit. We loved our families, in spite of the strong tendency of his father and my mother to interfere in our lives. And we wanted our children to know their grandparents, and other family members.

We moved some, wanting the right kind of country place for our children, and eventually settled in a rural area in the foothills of the Sierra, a place we found beautiful, and we established our home there.

We've had a very happy life. The conversation we began one night in Ridley's has never stopped. Our lives are coming to completion now. Chris, Ted, Nathan and Andy, our children, and their very dear spouses take amazingly good care of us. Their children do too. We are so full of love for them and so proud of the families that they have raised— good human beings, kind and loving. Bob and I cling tightly to each other these days, against the knowledge of inevitable separation, but we are also grateful knowing that we have already had more happiness than most people ever get.

Not long before she died, when my mother was in Sunrise Hospital in Las Vegas and knew she would not recover, mother said she wanted to tell me something important. In the hearing of one of our sons who was with us there in the ICU, my mother took my hand and told me that Bob had been the best husband and father anyone could want. She said she had been very wrong about him. "And," she said, "I'm sorry I didn't see it sooner." It was a sweet admission, and good to hear, though very long in coming.

My husband is eighty-five now. I am eighty. My tits hang down to my waist — but not my knees. Bob loves me still. And I love him. Grave and serious people accept natural phenomena. We find no fault with the law of gravity.

~0~

Sade Jones Nordgren Smith

OLD FAMILY DIVORCES

OLD FAMILY DIVORCES

<<>>

Dear Reader, unless you are a member of the family, you might want to skip this essay. It is filled with old family gossip – Even if you are a member of the family, you might not be interested in prattle. It's not salacious, just family drama.

The families my husband and I come from have a history of disastrous unions. I worked for a number of years as a registrar, researching the lineage of women wanting to join the Daughters of the American Revolution, and for some years after I retired from teaching, I volunteered as a genealogical aid at the Tulare County Library. Checking through old census records, one sees that in past centuries, so many women died in childbirth that a reasonably healthy man – who wasn't killed in war – would often outlive three wives, sometimes more.

Divorces were fewer in the old days, but women dying in childbirth were much more frequent, so marital break-ups were still high – just for a different reason. Might we conclude that our families had so many divorces because our women were too healthy to die? Not likely. But, it might be true. Both sides of our family have evidence of both female longevity and divorce.

To be serious, this essay is just a way to record some of the drama in the lives of our past family members. The stories my mother and other relatives told me so the history of our families isn't lost. We learn from the past, but only when we have a chance to know it. Most of the divorces are on my side of the family. There are no known family breakups in Bob's *deep* family history. But his family had two in more recent times. Both my husband's grandmothers divorced his grandfathers.

Here are their stories.

❂ Bob's father was Robert Mathews Ross. His mother was Henrietta Golembowski when she was born in 1887 in Indiana. She moved to Milwaukee, Wisconsin as a young girl and married Mathias Stanislaus Banaszynski. He had been born in Poland but came to America in early childhood. The couple had three children, but soon after the last child was born, (@1911), Henrietta, called Etta, divorced her husband and married a man named Rossi.

Her Banaszynski born children went to school using the surname Ross anglicized from Rossi, a common custom even today for recently immigrated people. Later, Etta divorced Rossi to remarry and divorce a number of times. She lived long, and was buried as Henrietta Pogorzelski.

There is nothing particularly noteworthy about this story. However, one awkward incident resulted from that first divorce. The incident happened to Bob's father during World War II, when he was a married man with children. It was to be a shock to his wife and him, and to cause money and inconvenience.

Bob's dad, Bob Ross, Sr. had been hired at Douglas Aircraft, in Santa Monica, California. It was a good job and paid well. One afternoon he arrived home after his shift to find his wife very nervous and two FBI agents were waiting in his living room. They sternly demanded to know *who* he was. World War 2 was raging. Security was tight during wartime. The FBI, especially near the defense industries, was diligently hunting spies and saboteurs. Douglas, where Bob Sr. was working was building planes for the war.

Bob's dad didn't pass the government vetting. He presented his discharge from the U.S. Navy. He presented his marriage certificate and his driver's license. The agents said that those documents didn't prove he was who he said he was. They informed him that there was no record of a Robert Mathews Ross ever having been born in the United States, so just who was he? It seems that Bob Sr.'s stepfather had never adopted him, so Robert Mathews Ross didn't legally exist.

Bob Sr. had to travel back to Milwaukee, and prove through afidavits by relatives, confirmed by school records, that he existed. When he finally became legal, Mattias Stanislaus Banaszynski Jr., his birth name was officially changed to Robert Mathews Ross. He could return to his family and job in California.

✪ Bob's other grandmother, Francis Miller Housdon, was a sweet natured, pious, Baptist woman born in Texas in 1892. She kept her vows and didn't believe in divorce until she was forced to file for one. It was during the fiftieth year of her marriage to Ivin Franklin Housdon, and it was at the urging of her daughter Ivy, and Francis' other two children, Lena and Kenneth.

Ivin, who had not lived with Francis for years, showed up one day with a contract and an eager buyer and wanted to sell her house. Francis had made all its payments by working in an old people's home, doing housework and ironing. She was seventy years old.

The divorce was long, long overdue. My mother-in-law, Ivy, told this story: When she was thirteen, the family lived in a tent city near Oildale, California. Ivin Housdon was working in the oilfields and making money in the fields. But one payday, after getting his paycheck, he took off with his work buddies. His wife and three children were stranded with no food or money. Ivy and her sister were forced to go to the families in other tents and beg milk and bread. He didn't return for over two weeks. It is a sad story. Ivy, her mother and younger sibs were not only deserted and hungry, but humiliated. My mother-in-law grew up to greatly appreciate a husband who was a responsible man, who didn't drink and did his best to take good care of his family.

✪   Now this history turns to my side of the family, with a more active history with the courts. (Some of these divorces happened in the 1800s, so an italicized 'line of descent' note will be added to aid reader clarity.) In 1846, an incident that led to divorce happened on in Nebraska, on The Oregon Trail. The divorce itself was later filed by Eli Michael, my father's great grandfather, to be free from his wife Nancy Frazier Michael (b. @ 1820). It was one of the very first divorces granted in the newly opened Oregon Territory.

What had caused the divorce happened along the Little Blue River in Nebraska, at an Oregon Trail Wagon Train encampment, Nancy, one of my father's great grandmothers, took a long look at the endless dusty and empty plain stretched out ahead of her. She told her husband that she was going back to Indiana where there was civilization and there were trees.

Nancy's husband Eli Michael refused to leave his parents, the rest of his big family, which included his brothers and their wives and children, or the grand adventure of the Trail. The alluring promise of a "land of milk and honey" that newspapers and magazines proclaimed would be free for all in Oregon's lush valleys awaited them.

Nancy was determined to go, and willing to travel by herself, but she demanded that she take the two smallest children, one not yet weaned, her clothing and personal possessions, and two of the horses. She told her older children they could choose to either go back to Indiana with her or to stay on the wagon train with their father. The older children chose to stay with Eli, their grandparents and the others who were bound for Brownsville, Oregon.

I find her heroic. It is easy to see how her frustrations could have come about. She was surrounded by her husband's family and far from her own. She was looking into bleak country, not the lush Indiana farm places that she had known. I'm not sure I could stand up to a wagon train full of Oregon bound, pre-Civil War Methodists, particularly in those paternalistic days. She was very brave to even imagine she could make the long trek home on her own.

Fortunately she didn't have to travel alone. When she and the two small children left, one of Eli's younger unmarried brothers volunteered to accompany Nancy and the children back home in safety. He did, and she and her two small daughters returned safely to Indiana and her own family.

(Line of descent: Nancy Frazier Michael > Mary Michael Harper > Isabelle Harper Stephenson > Waldo J. Stephenson > Sylvia Stephenson Ross.)

✪ The next family divorce, following chronological order, happened in 1883 in Atlanta, Georgia. This divorce was filed by Marion Josephine Roscoe Cox. (b. 1838) Josie, as she was called, was my Grandfather Cox's mother. Josie's father was a substantial plantation owner in Bossier Parish, Louisiana.

She and her sisters had been well educated and she became a music teacher in a seminary in the parish. When she married deputy sheriff Nathan F. Cox, the young couple first moved to New Orleans where he found a new job. But then, during the yellow fever epidemic, they fled with their children to Nathan's family home in Atlanta. They had four children. The two older died, and Josie took the two younger and fled back home to Bossier Parish, Louisiana.

By 1880, she had resumed teaching in the seminary, claiming to be a widow. She had left not only her husband, but his large extended family, just as Nancy Frazier Michael did.

There was a negative attitude about divorce in earlier centuries. This is probably the reason Josie listed herself as a *widow* when she reclaimed her family connections and her teaching job in Louisiana.

Records prove that she was not. She is listed as a widow on the 1880 Bossier Parish census, but returned to Atlanta some years that. She stayed just long enough to obtain an 1883 divorce. One doesn't divorce a dead man.

Once back in Lousiana, she left her teaching job and married her father's plantation manager, a man named Doyle. They had children together including a half-brother, Bert Doyle, whom my grandfather was very fond of and who eventually moved to California where my sibs and I knew him and his family.

(Line of descent: Marion Josephine Roscoe Cox > Ernest Bolden Cox > Sarah Ellen Cox Stephenson Stigmon > Sylvia Stephenson Ross)

The stories of Nancy Frazier Michael and Josie Roscoe Cox are an example that America is not a matrilineal society but it is a matrilocal one. Newly married couples tend to settle near the bride's family. These stories seem to prove that marriages work better if a woman isn't separated from her people. People doing genealogical research learn that newly married couples will often establish homes near the bride's family. American families are usually <u>patrilineal;</u> children will carry the husband's surname. But, they are likely to be <u>matrilocal;</u> families will settle near the wife's family.

Back in California, marital disasters continued to occur between 1895 and 1905.

My grandmother, Rena Jones Cox died when my mother, Sarah Cox, was four. Two of her aunts became very influential in Mama's life. The next two stories are about them. My mother was the child of an odd pairing, Ernest Cox, a 'southern gentleman' raised on a plantation, college educated, and his wife, Rena Jones Cox, who was half-Native American and had little schooling. Opposites do attract. (Through this Native grandmother, my mother's name is on the 1929 California State Indian Roll as is mine is on the 1950 California State Indian Roll, no. 30326.)

Each of the two aunts, who took the place of my mother's mother, came through her separate parents and were very different women. Both were named Sarah, though one would later change that name. Both would divorce. But one reflected the western pioneer ethos and hardships. The other reflected gracious southern living and a college degree when it wasn't common for women.

✪ The second of my mother's aunts to divorce a husband was <u>Sarah Elizabeth Jones Nordgren Smith,</u> (b. 1876.) She was half - California Indian. She was born beautiful. It is her picture that leads into this essay. Sarah Jones's neer-do-well father was a water witch and fiddler. He had a ranch in the foothills of the Sierra but wasn't very successful. Water witching and fiddling gave him popularity with the California pioneers who were his neighbors, but they brought in little money and his family was growing.

As the family's oldest daughter, by the time Sarah was four, she was doing housework and tending the babies. By the time she was seven, and old enough to go to school, Sarah was 'hired out' to a Swedish farmer who lived in another township. The man needed a helper for his pregnant wife on their remote farm. He couldn't pay for an adult housekeeper, but could pay Sarah's father a half rate for his child's labor.

The men came to agreement, and Sarah was bound out. She went with the farmer to work in his household. When she was fourteen, the Swede's wife died. Sarah was terrified to stay in his house after the man's wife's death. She ran away, walking and begging rides, back to her parents. She pleaded with them not to send her back. But any reader can predict what was to happen next. The Swede came after her. Her father listened to his pleas that his children needed Sarah. He sent her back with the man, in spite of his daughter's fearful appeals and his wife's tears.

By the time she was fifteen Sarah was pregnant by Mr. Nordgren. When this became apparent, neighborhood pressure forced the man to marry her. She was given no choice. The man who had raped her, shamed by her pregnancy, continued to treat her badly. She bore man's child a daughter. With the help of some neighboring farmers who sympathized with her, Sarah took her child and ran away.

Instead of going home to her parents, she found a wagon willing to transport her and her baby to the biggest city in the Central Valley, Fresno. Through a contact related to one of the neighbors who had helped her, Sarah found work as a cook in a boarding house. The couple that owned the house allowed her to keep her child. In addition to allowing her to keep her baby daughter with her, they helped her fill out the forms to file for divorce.

Sarah, though very young still, had remade herself. Now she renamed herself. Henceforth she wanted to be called Sade. She had a good job with good people. But she was too pretty not to be noticed. She soon was courted by a couple of the boarders, a man who was a violin teacher and another, a quiet, hard-working blacksmith. She chose the latter, a man named George L. Smith. His business boomed. He expanded the shop, going from fabricating wagon wheels to working on trucks and cars as time passed. Sade went from being the uneducated daughter of a barn dance fiddler/water witch, to being the wife of a prosperous businessman in Fresno, the biggest city in the Central Valley.

Sade and George shared a long, comfortable life together. Besides a spacious home in Fresno, they bought a ranch up at Shaver Lake for summers. Sarah Jones Nordgren now Sade Smith went on to have more children with George, and in addition to her own children, she and her husband adopted two boys. She fought my grandfather for court custody of my mother, who lived in her for about four years.

By the time I was a child, due to his illness, Aunt Sade

and Uncle George sold the summer ranch in the mountains where my mother had spent many summers, but their home on Thesta Street in Fresno was a favorite place for my sister Nancy and I. Later, after George's death, Aunt Sade lived with her daughter Lois Smith Traber in the Tower District. My sister Nancy was married from Lois's home on Peralta Street, in Fresno, with Lois as a witness.

(line of descent: collateral, Sarah Jones Smith, sister of Rena Jones Cox > Sarah Cox Stephenson Stigmon > Sylvia Stephenon Ross)

✪   I can trigger a mental visit with my mother's *other* Aunt Sarah whenever I turn on Turner Classic Movies and see Ethel Barrymore appearing in an old film. Sarah Roscoe Cox Ricketts Justice, (b. 1877 in Atlanta) was very proper and elegant in her demeanor. Born in Georgia, she was raised on a Louisiana plantation. She would eventually travel to Los Angeles, then to England, then back to America to settle in Glendale, California.

She was the daughter of Marion Josephine Roscoe Cox Doyle, 'Josie,' mentioned earlier. My grandfather Ernest and his sister Sarah attended private schools in the Shreveport area of Louisiana. Then they both attended college at Baylor in Waco, Texas, where their maternal aunt was married to a prominent judge.

Sarah's brother Ernest earned an engineering certificate and enlisted in the Spanish American war. Sarah earned a diploma from Baylor with a major in music while my grandfather was in the army.

Upon graduation, Sarah married. She and her husband soon had three children, but the marriage did not go well. But since her mother had been divorced, Sarah Cox Ricketts knew she had an option. She gave up her two sons to her ex-husband, and she kept custody of her daughter.

In the meanwhile, her brother Ernest had been scarred and partially blinded after brain surgery in an army hospital in Jackson, Florida. Upon discharge, he'd received a lifetime pension. The sister and brother's mother had died, and Ernest, now visually handicapped and suffering migraine type headaches, had no desire to return to Louisiana. In the new century, 1900, he caught a train to balmy Southern California.

Now divorced, Sarah stayed for a time in Louisiana, then took her baby daughter Viola Roscoe Ricketts and her divorce decree, and she followed her brother to Los Angeles. By that time, around 1906, Ernest and my grandmother Rena were married. They had room in their home for Sarah and little Viola Roscoe.

Los Angeles was a very fashionable place to live at that particular time. Easterners were moving west and building winter homes there. The film industry was just getting started and so was aviation. Its good climate made it ideal for investors in both areas.

Sarah soon found a well-paying and respectable job playing the piano in an elite gentlemen's club in Los Angeles during afternoon tea. The club welcomed a woman of refinement and education. It was a secure position and my handicapped grandfather, who could not work in the daytime or in bright lights with his handicap, could watch little Viola if his wife couldn't. Sarah was able to earn enough to help support herself and her daughter.

My mother was named for this aunt and this story has a happy ending. In Los Angeles, Sarah met and married a rather wealthy, widowed Englishman. He was an importer/exporter by trade and widowed. They married. Sarah and her daughter traveled with him by train and then ship to England. They lived there in comfort until the late nineteen thirties. Sarah's daughter, Viola Roscoe, attended Queen Anne's School. When Sarah's husband retired from business, the three of them returned to the United States, and bought a home in Glendale, California.

(line of descent: collateral, Sarah Cox Ricketts Justice, sister of Ernest Bolden Cox > Sarah Cox Baird Stebbins Stephenson Stigmon > Sylvia Stephenson Ross)

More marital drama was to occur in my mother's own generation. Two cousins that my mother loved, the daughters of her aunts Sade and Sarah, divorced husbands. My mother did too. Among them, the three women, Lois Smith Traber, Viola Ricketts Fenton, and my mother Sarah Cox Baird Stebbins Stephenson, Stigmon collected two annulments and eight divorces between 1923 and 1958.

✪   My mother, Sarah Cox, first eloped with Ray Baird, a young law student. She had been living in the too indulgent custody of her Aunt Sade. My mother was just fifteen. The marriage was quickly annulled. She finished high school with a court-appointed foster family who were friends of my grandfather. It was difficult and there was gossip, but she was a good student and earned a scholarship to nursing school.

During her third year of nurses' training at the prestigious Stanford-Lane Hospital in Oakland, my mother dropped out of the nursing program to marry a man named Stebbins and move to Los Angeles. I know little about him.

A few years after her divorce from Stebbins, my mother married my father, Waldo James Stephenson, a older, childless widower. That marriage ended eleven months later with his death in February of 1937. Her marriage to my stepfather, Joseph Stigmon, ended in his death in November of 1954.

It seems sad to me that my mother's longest marriage was to last just fifteen years. If we live until mid-June of this year, Bob and I will have been married sixty years. My husband and I know how fragile relationships can be, and how lucky we have been. Our hope for our descendants is that they will have long, happy, and loving unions as we have. But should any find themselves in an intolerable situation, we hope that they never feel any shame at leaving a destructive marriage.

~0~

a day with

Mother's Aunt May

A DAY WITH MOTHER'S AUNT MAY

<<>>

Aunt May was my maternal grandmother Rena's younger sister. I'd disqualified May Jones Anderson Collard in my earlier essay on divorces in the family. May didn't quite fit in. She wasn't divorced. She had been widowed during World War One. But her story is good for telling. She, like Rena and Sade, was half Indian. And May had to learn to manage on her own.

When I was very small, before my sibs were born, my mother was having her own troubles with widowhood and her relationship with the married man who would become my stepfather. I was very young when I was taught to call the man "Daddy." During those difficult years, my mother would take me up into the Central Valley of California and leave me with my grandfather on his ranch for various periods of time, but not longer than two weeks.

It was a long drive, five hours or more in those old days to travel by car from West L.A. to Madera. Grandpa's ranch had chickens and a cow, and a good dog named Boy who was as tall as I.

I loved my grandfather as much as I did my mother, and I also loved the clean smell of the country. So though I missed my mother, I was happy in the country with my Grandpa.

One morning, long after we'd had our oatmeal and coffee, I was outdoors playing with Boy. My mother's Aunt May came to Grandpa's ranch in her truck. She had come to take me to her own ranch where she lived alone. She was going to haul a calf to the slaughterhouse and said she thought I'd enjoy going with her. I'd met her before, and knew she was part of my family. I didn't know her well, but I understood about relatives and wasn't afraid to go somewhere for a day with Aunt May. Undoubtedly, her motivation to take a three and a half-year-old along with her for hours was that my grandfather needed a break from me. Hitching down and up my overalls every time I needed to use the outhouse and keeping me out of the ditch by the road must have been fatiguing for a man in his sixties.

That morning with Aunt May, I walked with my back straight and didn't complain when I had to give up barefoot freedom and wear shoes. I felt like I was going to be Aunt May's helper. I liked her truck. When we got to her ranch, we went out to the small barn behind her house, and I walked with her as she led the calf from its small pen. I tried to match her stride.

"Now, hon, hold the ramp steady," I remember her saying.

I gripped the splintery wood of the truck's ramp with with my fingers. I probably didn't weigh thirty-five pounds, and couldn't have been much help, but I felt a grand pride because she was depending on me to keep the ramp from wobbling as the calf was shoved up into the bed of the truck. When we got to the slaughterhouse, I didn't have to help. Some men came out to the truck, greeted my aunt, and took the calf out to a place behind the big building. The building didn't look like a barn, more like one of the city buildings near the apartment where I lived with my mother. But it stood alone here, looking out of place in empty fields, without other buildings around it.

It began to get hot as the morning moved along. My aunt and I waited in the shade of the building and watched while the calf was hoisted, bled, gutted, skinned, and taken to hang in the big slaughterhouse. When we took a drink from a hose beside its wall, my mother's aunt dipped her hands in the water before she turned the faucet off. She wiped my forehead and cheeks,

"There, Baby, that feels cool now, don't it?" she asked. I didn't answer, just nodded. I wasn't insulted. My mother called me Baby too. It didn't mean I was one.

I followed her into the building. The inside was dark and we had been in the sun. It took a while to be able to see. I stood in the doorway. The slaughterhouse's windows were small and high up. They let little light into the place. I listened as my aunt told the worker the way she wanted the meat packaged for the locker. She and the worker smoked cigarettes while they talked. Aunt May looked small next to the slaughterhouse man and she made him laugh. They weren't talking about the calf anymore.

I still listened, but they weren't talking about my mother, my grandfather or me, so I wandered away, deeper into the shadowy interior space of the slaughterhouse. I wasn't afraid and I was curious. I walked close to the swinging meat that used to be Aunt May's calf, and at first, I couldn't even tell what it was though she had pointed it out to me as we entered.

Slowly, I could sort of work out the calf in the skinless, upside down carcass hanging there. I didn't know where its head or feet and skin had gone. As I looked beyond it, I saw that in the shadowy building there were other carcasses hanging further down the row, other people's calves.

I became aware how much I didn't like the smell of the

building. It wasn't good, but it wasn't as bad as our garbage cans in the alley behind our apartment smelled before the garbage truck came.

I wanted to go back outside and run over to the stock pens where the air was bright, warmer, and smelled better. I liked watching the live animals better than the dead ones. I'd determined that while cow smell wasn't good, slaughterhouse smell was worse. Aunt May said, "You can go on. Just stay where I can see you." She and the man came to the doorway and watched me running around tossing bits of hay into the pens and running back if one of the cows there came close to the fence and me. I didn't worry about the cows breaking out through the fence. I knew that Aunt May and the slaughterhouse man would protect me.

The year was 1940. I didn't know it then. I didn't think in designated units of time more precise than *before, after, pretty soon,* and *in a day or two.* I was just learning the seasons. I didn't quite know if it was spring or summer. Weeds were turning brown in the fields, but the bales of hay in my grandfather's barn had some green. It was hot in the day but cold at night. The cues my mother had taught me for seasons weren't very solid.

It was shady and lush with trees down by the San

Joaquin River where we stopped on the way back to Aunt May's ranch. We got out of the truck to eat a picnic of cheese, bread, and soda under the willows.

At the river, the air was sweet and pushed the smell of cows, the slaughterhouse, and the truck's gasoline smell out of my nose. There weren't any field butterflies here away from the pastures, but there were mosquitos buzzing near the water. If we stayed in the sun, the mosquitoes didn't bite us. Aunt May drew a line in the dirt from one tree to another with her heel, and forbade me to go past it. That was all right. I didn't want to get near the deep and swift river.

When I asked, she told me that the beautiful orange and blue creatures zipping around over the water were dragonflies. I didn't know the word dragon, so thought the insects' name was because they seemed to be dragging their long tail-bodies behind them like train cars. We squatted down on a low-slung willow branch to eat. The sodas had gotten warm in the truck waiting for us to finish at the slaughterhouse. They foamed over and made our hands sticky, but we were thirsty and they tasted good.

My aunt left me to brace herself on a tree. She bent down to dip her handkerchief in the river water. I was afraid she would fall and disappear under the green water. She didn't. We cleaned our hands with the damp handkerchief before we got back in the truck.

Aunt May wore jeans and shirts like a man. She was skinnier and older than my mother, but younger than my mother's other aunts. Mama told me that her Aunt May had been the baby of the Jones family. She moved quicker than women usually did. When she climbed into the calf's pen to put a halter on him, she moved with more speed than I'd ever seen my grandfather move. My mother thought men were better at doing everything. I knew I was going to be a woman when I grew up, not a man. I wanted to do things like Aunt May — drive a truck instead of a coupe, sling a lasso over a calf's neck, and climb in and out of pens faster than men could.

Most people I knew had a radio in their homes. Grandpa didn't. He had a pump and a windmill, a dog, chickens and a Jersey cow, but he didn't have electric lights or a radio. He sang country songs and hymns as he worked and he taught me the tunes and words. Aunt May had a big radio, bigger and louder than the one in our apartment at home. She listened to music that made me feel happy. She told me to nap when we came home, but then she turned the radio on.

I slipped off the sofa. She didn't make me go back to lie down again. She danced with me until we were both tired, and then we both took a nap on her tall iron bed in her sweet-smelling room.

That was the only day I was ever to spend with my mother's Aunt May. I've never forgotten it. It stays in my mind so clearly that I can still smell the slaughterhouse and the river, and even the fragrance of the toiletries on the big mirrored dressing table in her bedroom. She wasn't my mother's favorite aunt. She kept too busy doing things our mother would never do like raising calves. But, once, not until I was around eleven, my mother sounded sympathetic to her. She told my sister and me that Aunt May had loved a man named George Collard. She waited for him while he was in prison. George's health had broken down while he was there, and he came back a sick man.   Mama only told us because we'd been in the room and overheard her cousin Lois telling her about it. It had shocked my sister Nancy and me to know our family knew someone who went to prison.

Nancy confronted mother about it. Mother explained that May was a good and loyal woman. She had known George since before he had his troubles. He'd wanted to marry her, but if she married him she'd lose the pension she had from her first husband. Mother said she didn't know if they were *legally* married or not. "You girls are not supposed to think George was a bad person," she added. "He was just someone who had made a mistake."

I asked what he had done, and she said he was a bookkeeper who embezzled money from his boss. May was able to build a house for them up in the hills of the Sierra doing most of the physical work herself. They used the money from the sale of her Madera ranch to buy the property, and George told her exactly what to do from a hammock strung between two of the pines. It took mother's Aunt May two years to finish the house. They lived together for the rest of his life, and she took good care of him until he died.

Mother and we children visited her once there in around 1953. I was in the house she built. It was tidy and had a parlor, bedroom, kitchen, bathroom, and laundry. It was very clean inside, in spite of the pines' pitchy litter outside. The pitch was something in addition to the wildlife that made my mother and Nancy prefer city life.

On that day, Aunt May served my mother, Nancy and me strong tea from a chipped blue enamel coffee pot. Theresa, just a baby still, sat on the linoleum floor with her toys. Our brothers were busy out under the pine trees and exploring the creek.

I wouldn't see mother's aunt May again until she was over eighty. I was married and our children were in school by then. May was older but little changed. She was still skinny and still favored jeans and a plaid shirt. But now, George Collard had been gone for years and her only child had also died. She had given up the mountains she loved. She didn't remember taking me to the slaughterhouse or our picnic. Perhaps, as Gabriel Garcia Marquez wrote: *"The heart's memory eliminates the bad and magnifies the good."* The ranch out by the river that I remembered so pleasantly from my early childhood must have been a sad and lonely place for her while she waited for her husband to finish his sentence, a place she might want to forget.

However, she remembered well the occasion in the early nineteen fifties when my mother, Nancy and I had coffee with her. I was on the brink of being a woman; Nancy was coming along right behind me, already worried about clothes and make-up. Being a woman was considered a significant achievement on its own by my mother's aunts. It didn't have to come with beauty, skills or any particular talents. But I wished Aunt May had remembered that day when we took the calf to the slaughterhouse, had a picnic by the river, and danced until we were tired.

Before we left, she told us again that she missed her

mountains, but that she was too old to live where she wanted. "I have to live where people can find my corpse when I drop down dead," she said with a droll grin. She lit another cigarette and winked to let us know she wasn't planning on dying all that soon.

I'm sorry that we lived so far away and I'd not had more time to be with her. I looked her up on public records when I was doing some genealogical work. On the 1930 voter index, she is entered as Ellen M. Collard. It was the only public record I found. She listed her ethnicity as Indian. I like that when filling out the form she chose her mother's ethnicity over her father's. I know his life was hard back in 1883, but feel a grudging resentment that her father sent his first daughter out to work as a young child — and not to school.

Nancy and I were fond of our great aunts. It is sad that our sister Theresa was born too late to actually have known them. Of our great aunts, I most loved Aunt Sade. She was the kindest person I ever knew. I knew her best of the three, knew that she liked the kind of people my sisters and brothers and I would someday be. Sade Smith found jobs for Indian women, whose parents and grandparents she'd known in the mountains and as a girl. She took in any stray in the family who needed her. She eased my childhood burdens because I knew that if it ever got so bad at home that I could bring myself to leave my mother and sisters and brothers, I would go to her.

Alas, I am not like her. I'm not a warm or friendly person. I don't like people around me all the time. It shames me to admit that my charities are only of the checkbook variety, but it is true.

But while Aunt Sade was the aunt I most loved, the aunt I most admired was mother's Aunt Sarah. If I could have made myself into her, I would have. I still would.   I learned to play the piano as she did, and I've read all of Shakespeare's plays and sonnets. I've even read Bertrand Russell's essays, and G. B. Shaw's plays, volumes on the bookshelves in her house. Now, when such intellectual endeavors have passed me, I buy Brit series DVDs that remind me of Aunt Sarah and her years in England. I try to stand straight and don't wear fingernail polish. I twist my hair up as she did.

Yet, we are who we are, not whom we want to be. My hair won't twist into a thick curly silver knot and spin out to form a glistening halo around my face. It is straight and lank. Instead of looking like Ethel Barrymore, I look more like a bankside woman from the movie *Deliverance*, a little raw and tattered, but one who could build a house.

One has to be born with Aunt Sarah's resonant and commanding presence to be able to sing her songs. Their music plays in my ears, but I can't get the lyrics right. To my mother's great and oft spoken regret, Aunt May of the calf pen, river and pine litter, is the aunt I am like. Like her, I don't respect convention. Like her, I prize personal loyalties above obedience to the law. And, like her, I am tenacious in loving.

Mother's Aunt May taught me that a woman could do anything a man could do. It just might take her a little longer. When I pick up a pry bar or post-hole digger, and I know how to use it, I think of that woman wearing jeans and a work shirt, using her own hands to build a livable house back in the 1940s and 50s. There weren't so many power tools available then. Nails were pounded in with a carpenter's hammer, not a nail gun. One used one's wrist to turn a screwdriver. It didn't come with a power cord or a battery. I'd have waited years for my man if he were in jail, just as she did — whether he and I were married or not, and whether he was guilty of a crime or not. A whimsy occurs to me, a little glance into genetics. Maybe mother's Aunt May never really did die. Maybe none of us do, as long as our species stays alive, our essence pops up here and there in some new person.

~0~

THE GOD

OF

MATHEMATICS

142

THE GOD OF MATHEMATICS

<<>>

This essay is the last in the book for a good reason. People, many of them my friends, may find it offensive. If you are serious practitioner of religion, you surely won't like it. Close the book here, knowing I respect our differences and don't want to offend you.

I've had an extremely lucky life. Ever since I was seventeen, things have gone very well for me. I know how rare this is, and am appreciative of this unusual good fortune. My gratitude goes to the good people who have been the agents of my good fortune. They are the people who brought me the gift of hope when I was a child. They are also the people who helped me build a life that has been so much better than so many other people's lives on this earth that I feel "survivor's guilt" today.

I have enjoyed living very much and don't want my life to stop. Belief in life after death is a seductive attraction. However, I'm not very seducible. No matter how appealing the lure of an after-life concept might be, I can't believe in it, any more than I can believe in a personal, caring god. I don't believe we go on, morphed into an invisible state of being. And that's okay.

It is impossible for my kind of logic to conceive of an afterlife. Our minds are a function of our brains, and when our bodies decay, our minds cease to function. This happens even when we are injured or ill in a way that critically upsets our neurological systems. There has never been any empirical data that can prove otherwise.

Neither can I thank god for this lucky life of mine. The only god that I could believe in wouldn't be a petty once-upon-a-time potentate like a King of the Assyrians or Caliph of the Turks. My god would never grant favor to one 'blessed' person while ignoring billions of others with the same exact needs and wants. I wish others well, but I don't pray for them or myself. It seems such a basically selfish act: "Gimme, gimme, God." "Don't worry about those billions of others who are suffering from cancer in the same way my friend is, God, just cure my friend."

My god doesn't do that kind of thing. It isn't the kind of god who would 'have his reasons' to tornado a little Baptist church in mid-America or tsunami thousands of people in Asia just going about their business. Nope. My kind of god is impersonal. It has no gender. It has no sons, mothers, or prophets. It isn't very involved with ants or bees or mammals like me.

When I was seventeen, I planned to give my life over to God's service. I'd been educated in Catholic schools. I found them places of security. School was a place where if I only behaved, I would be treated well. It was something I had not known in my family home. No one ever hit, kicked, or cursed me in school.

And, best, there were no men in school other than Mr. Cooper who swept the classrooms after school, and he brought a bucket of sawdust if anyone threw up. Although I was attracted to men, I had early on learned to be so fearful of them, that I stayed close to the nearest door whenever I was confined in a room with one. In high school, I wouldn't let the nice Catholic boys I dated touch me except on the dance floor and then I trembled from fear, not excitement. Going into a convent after graduation meant I'd never have to be afraid.

There was another reason why I wanted to be a nun, a more important reason. My decision was the result of my long doubt over the existence of a personal god.

As a five-year-old, I was shy with the nuns and even with other children, but I was spellbound by the first grade *Bible* charts and the wondrous stories that came with the charts. It wasn't only the *Bible*. Sister Mary Viator also told us about the saints and the wondrous miracles they performed in those olden times. I listened with rapt pleasure. But I'd already confirmed that the Santa, whose lap I sat on at the Broadway Department Store, had dry glue on his upper lip. By my sixth birthday, I'd learned to be cynical. I knew what grown-ups told me wasn't necessarily the truth.

By second grade, I was a total skeptic. Sister Theresa Josephine told us dogs and cats couldn't go to heaven because they didn't have souls. "Only people have souls." she said, and she went on to say that souls are invisible. *Invisible* bothered me. Electricity and germs were invisible and they were true. But ghosts and witches and monsters under my bed were invisible and they weren't true. Souls, like the devil and god, seemed more like the things that weren't true.

I learned every Bible story and every lesson in **The Baltimore Catechism,** and though I had a poor rote memory, I tried my best to memorize every prayer I was expected to recite. I said prayers, as often as any child in a bad situation could, hoping that I was wrong, and there was an invisible god who would save me.

Then, in high school, we studied apologetics (a branch of theology devoted to the defense of the divine origin and authority of Christianity). The girls on my track and I learned the countering answers to anyone who denied the truth of Christianity and Catholicism. I didn't deny those conjoined 'C's', but I didn't believe in them either. To further complicate my spiritual life, "God, the Father" was a phrase I heard continually. The only kind of father I'd ever known was the one in my home and not appealing.

I talked over my doubts with the priest in the confessional and my sister advisor. Both the priest and nun told me the same thing. My doubts came from pride and were the work of the devil. But where does a devil fit in? If one has trouble believing in god, she would hardly believe in a devil. I could believe science. Electricity turned on the lights in the house. Germs gave my sister and brother chickenpox a week after I'd brought them home from school. God's miracles were not as dependable. I smile, now that I'm eighty. But at fifteen and sixteen, I was too serious to see this in a humorous way.

The ultimate argument, the one that kept me going to mass and spending time on my knees in the school's chapel was this single one: All those theologians and leaders of the church were so much smarter than I ever would be, how could I not accept what they found believable and true?

I tried and tried again. I'd read **Seven Storey Mountain** by Thomas Merton and listened to priests arguing from the pulpit over Pierre Teilhard de Chardin's commentaries. Between my sophomore and senior years at Conaty, I must have read Francis Thompson's poem, *The Hound of Heaven*, about a thousand times, and not just for its literary value.

> I fled Him, down the nights and down the days;
> I fled Him, down the arches of the years;
> I fled Him, down the labyrinthine ways
> Of my own mind; and in the mist of tears
> I hid from Him, and under running laughter...

I tried, because, yes. All those theologians and great leaders of the church *were* smarter than I, and they believed.

That realization sent me straight from high school graduation to the novitiate of the Sisters of Mercy. I wanted to be surrounded by the belief I did not feel, to have a wall to protect me from my aberrant mind. I wanted that questioning, non-accepting mind contained. Then it wouldn't destroy what had been the safest and best part of my life, my Catholic school life.

Even music I cherished was related to Christianity. I'd

passed the auditions to sing with an honored high school choir and with the Loyola University Mixed Choir. Though never with a soloist's timbre or resonance, I had the competence to sing with a church choir all my life. But apostates do not get to sing in church choirs. Atheists are not invited to enjoy the grand and elegant experience of attending a solemn high mass and singing Bach to the smells of incense and bees' wax candles burning and the sights of ceremonial processionals in a beautiful church with a vaulted ceiling.

I'd also been taught to feel guilty because I cared so much about giving up the *pleasures of mortal delights* – singing and enjoying friendships and loving my siblings, even being asked to dances. I knew I wasn't keeping my thoughts on godliness the way a good Catholic girl should. In the summer of 1954, I left home and entered a medieval and monastic life in the convent to protect myself from disbelief.

The novitiate was in a part of the motherhouse of the sisters in Burlingame, California. It was an impressive building situated on forty acres of wooded hillside. Hallways, administrative offices and parlors opened to each side of the foyer, but the central panneled doors directly opposite the entrance led to the chapel which was larger than many churches. Because open interior courtyards of the building flanked each side, the vaulted chapel was bright. Its beautiful stained-glass windows let in light throughout the day. Boxing the courtyards were long wings providing lodging for the residents.

The building was on a hill and the slope allowed a daylight basement as large as the upper stories. The lower floor held the refectories for dining and the kitchens, recreation rooms. It had a laundry for small hand-wash items complete with sinks and irons that weren't electric but had to be heated on a gas stove. Large storage areas were in the basement also. There were no phones except in the administrative offices, no radios or TVs to be seen anywhere. There was an absolute quiet, and that was welcoming.

The novitiate was to the left side of the central chapel. Its right side was reserved for professed nuns who were in residence — the teachers for Mercy High School, which was also on the forty wooded acres property. A number of very elderly or ill nuns lived there also.

The garments we were given were similar to what I'd seen nuns wearing, but without the starched white coif or wimple around the face, and with only a simple veil. We were given white cotton underpants with legs covered nearly to the knees, no bras but vests made of white cotton, long sleeved black shirts, cape-lets and petticoats, sturdy cloth belts to go over the petticoats but under the outer skirts, black stockings and shoes.

I found that a pocket watch was attached to the belt assigned to my use, as were cords from which dangled a pair of small scissors in a leather case. The skirts had slits at the sides too allow us to retrieve items from the pocket and belt as needed. We were given the clothes and told that a word implying ownership did not belong in a nun's vocabulary. We were to use the expression "to my use," rather than "my."

When I changed from the clothes I was wearing, I found that the postulant's skirt pocket held a handkerchief, rosary, and a petite leather-bound copy of *Imitation of Christ*, a book familiar to me. It was written by a monk who lived from 1380 until 1471, Thomas à Kempis. We would find a Bible, Missal, and Hymnal at our assigned kneeler in chapel. There was to be a small library available to us. It housed devotional books as well as many editions of the Bible.

Every day was ordered by bells and buzzers. They rang with different sounds for different purposes. We had a schedule of classes and chores, and sound kept us aware of time, though we had pocket watches which we scarcely needed. We were silent in our work, and always on time.

Most of our days would fall under general silence rules. The most that was spoken aloud was a murmured, *"Benedicamus Dominum,"* said by the more senior of the women passing in a hallway, followed by the more junior woman's soft response, *"Deo Gracias."*

Actual conversation was restricted to a forty-minute period in the evening between supper and vespers. We stitched and mended priestly vestments, altar cloths or darned our stockings. Once every few weeks we were given paper to write a letter home, but no envelopes. One of the sisters would pick up our letters at the end of the recreation period. They were to be addressed and mailed to our families from our novice mistress's office.

Strange as it is, I found myself very happy in the novitiate. It was quiet. I couldn't remember a time when I hadn't lived with explosions of angry drama. If schools had been a refuge five days a week, 8 to 3, through my school years, the novitiate was an all day, all night, every day refuge. There were no harsh words spoken. There were hardly any words spoken at all. We prayed, worked and took classes. I still remember formulae from a class in minor logic, *"...barbara celerent darii ferio."* But alas, I've forgotten the applications, though not the way a syllogism is set.

We also took a class in Mariology, the study of Mary's role in the Bible and in early literature. And, last, we had to take typing. I had been assigned to a college prep/arts track in high school. It allowed no space for a typing class.

The nuns of the order were either nurses or teachers. Either occupation demanded familiarity with the typewriter. I managed to do well in the first two classes, but failed typing. I couldn't make the speed required. I was expected to find time in the virtually non-existent 'free' time we were allowed for study, bathing, or praying, and sign in on a time sheet for a practice period every day but Sunday. It didn't help.

I was aware that I had a birth defect that shortened and weakened my left little finger. I asked to be allowed to not use that finger at all and type with my nine good fingers. The nun in charge denied my petition. Her logic was that since my history in the office files indicated that I could play the piano with all ten fingers, I ought to be able to type with all ten, not nine. However, I never could sufficiently depress the Q, W, A, S, and Z keys using ten fingers.

A few years later, in another life, when I'd taken maternity leave from my job to await our first son's birth, my husband pulled out his typewriter and set me to work practicing with nine fingers. I learned to type easily. Although there had been some logic to what the teaching sister demanded, a typewriter is not a piano. They have different pressure demands. The longer keyboard on a piano allows for a more flexible wrist movement. This episode was a very minor annoyance, a petty thing to remember now at the end of my life. I *only* remember it because I was to spend much of my teaching and writing life using the typewriter or computer's keyboard.

In general, I was very happy leading a nun's life. Certainly, it was easier than the drudgery and fear of my home. I missed my mother, whom I loved as children can love a parent. I very much missed my sisters and brothers and friends. I received few letters, but one leaves communication with the external world when one enters a convent. I didn't expect mail. Meditation and prayer became time for reflection and thought.

As time went on, my own thoughts on god's nature surfaced even stronger with time and reflection. I had not been protected from apostasy. I stopped believing entirely, and consequently began to feel an enormous peace, a tranquility of mind. I had finally accepted my non-belief.

I wanted to continue to live a nun's life: orderly, quiet, busy, and morally circumscribed. I was cheerful and comfortable in that life. But I felt such so dishonest, and without the honesty of a true commitment to a kind of god I didn't believe in, I couldn't stay. It would hypocritical and self-serving.

I'd grown intellectually during the long periods of silence. I had come to see that the world was filled with many people much smarter than I—and they were intellectually equal to Catholic theologians. Not all of them believed in a loving, punishing, Christian god either.

Later I would find there was a whole philosophic movement that thought as I did. But I didn't yet know Ralph Waldo Emerson. I had not read of his theological arguments in the Divinity School at Harvard. The 18th century Enlightment period in history hadn't been taught in the classrooms where I had studied. I only knew that I didn't believe what Christians were expected to believe, what nuns, novices, and postulants were expected to believe. At seventeen, living in a convent, on my knees in chapel, I broke away from everything I'd been taught.

It would prove quite difficult to leave the novitiate. When I asked for an appointment with my novice mistress, I was made to wait and then postponed.

156

When finally, I met with her and explained why I wanted to leave, I was told that the devil was tempting me and dismissed to chapel to pray.

I waited a week and made an appointment again hoping that my request would be taken more seriously. This time I was deferred for a longer time, and the third time, I was told I needed to discuss this with my confessor. My novice mistress said that she, and the other nuns teaching us, felt I was adjusting to the life very well. Of course, that was true. I did like the life. God was the problem, not the convent.

The priest came two afternoons a month. I waited and explained my problem to him. He said the same thing that Mother Eleanor had said, suggesting that the devil was taking advantage of my homesickness.

My request still wasn't taken seriously, and I began to feel trapped. I'd have recurring nightmares for years that I'd be running through yards and down streets trying to get to a railroad. Why the dream had a railroad, I have no idea. I'd come to the novitiate in a car, and when I left I was in a plane on an early morning flight out of the San Francisco Airport.

The problem was solved for me within a month. My stepfather died. It was evening. I was called to the phone in the office. The novice mistress stood near me to monitor my conversation with my mother. After I said what I could to comfort my mother, I told her I was coming home.

I was allowed to talk a short while more, then motioned to hang up the phone. The novice mistress then led me through the labyrinthine maze of the rooms on the professed sisters' side of the building, took me upstairs to a nun's empty cell, a tiny room with a crucifix and a bed, down a dim corridor. She told me where the nearest lavatory was should I need it, and told me to wait. She left, came back with a nightgown, pointed to a hook on the wall for my clothing, and told me I was to sleep there. She would see to me in the morning.

The novice mistress came to the room when it was still dark. She had the suitcase that I had brought the day I entered the novitiate with the clothes I had worn. A sister brought in a cup of coffee and a roll. Then the two nuns rode with me to the San Francisco Airport in a limo driven by one of the groundsmen.

My mother met me later that morning at LAX. It all took place so quickly. I remember feeling strange in civilian clothing. I was so happy to see my sisters and brothers and in spite of their father's death, they were happy to see me.

The oldest daughter of a big family knows what family life is about. She usually wants to have either no children or many children. With my sibs around me, I realized I was the latter, and that leaving the novitiate opened up the option to have children of my own.

For weeks, I didn't have the courage to tell my mother why I left, that I no longer held to any religious belief. I knew she was disappointed in me. I think she had liked saying she had a daughter who was studying to become a nun. It held a sort of maternal Catholic panache, equivalent to a Jewish mother saying, "My son is in medical school." However, now she was distracted by my stepfather's burial and having to run his business affairs. I was there to help. I just stopped going to mass. I felt better than I had during all my years of questioning. One needs a far better imagination than I to believe in a personal god. When I did tell my mother, I'd had my eighteenth birthday. She wasn't happy, and told me that as long as I lived under her roof, I wasn't to say anything like this again. I didn't. I was the most compliant of daughters, but that didn't make me a believer.

A couple of my friends from school were involved in the church's young singles club, and when they invited me to go with them. I did. Another good friend had the contacts to arrange an interview for me with Walt Disney Productions in Burbank. I took a batch of drawings I'd made in high school. Soon I had a driver's license and a job I liked. I'd become an adult. I was free. I was raised with religion, but it didn't suit the person I was born.

Our kind of primate is very good at thinking things up. We create monsters in the sea, trolls under the bridge, fairies and angels, spirits and saints, devils and any number of gods with conflicting rules. I hold to a fanciful concept of something I heard or read somewhere. It is called the god of mathematics, a brilliance going beyond infinities of universes. It connects everything—from music to DNA strands, from radio waves to space travel. It needs nothing from us. It needs no praise. It needs no blame. This god doesn't even need the awe I feel in my observation of its connective expanse. It is my spiritual fantasy, no better or worse than anyone else's.

I follow a way of life that holds one single commandment sacred: *Do unto others as you would have them do unto you.* It is what my mother-in-law practiced, and it is incorporated as a tenet of wisdom in nearly all religions. I try my best to live by its rule, as she did.

~ fin ~

Beverly Richardson's Book Recommendations:

Byatt, A.S.
Possession

Cherian, Anne
A Good Indian Wife

Desai, Kirian
Inheritance of Loss

Dunn, Katherine
Geek Love

Eugenides, Jeffrey
Middlesex

George, Elizabeth
Playing for the Ashes, et al.

Golden, Peter
Wherever There is Light

Gruen, Sara
Water for Elephants

Hornby, Nick
How To Be Good

Hoseini, Kahled
    A Thousand Splendid Suns

Hurston, Zora Neale
    Their Eyes were Watching God

Irving, John
    A Son of the Circus, et al.

Kingsolver, Barbara
    The Poisonwood Bible, et al.

Lahiri, Jhumpa
    The Namesake

Patchett, Ann
    Bel Canto

Roberts, Gregory David
    Shantaram

Robinson, Marilynn
    Housekeeping

Roy, Arundhati
    The God of Small Things

Rushdie, Salman
    Midnight's Children

Smiley, Jane
A Thousand Acres

Smith, Zadie
White Teeth

Stephenson, Neal
Cryptonomicon, et al.

Strout, Elizabeth
Olive Kitteridge

Toole, John Kennedy
A Confederacy of Dunces

Tyler, Anne
If Morning Ever Comes, et al.

Updike, John
Rabbit, Run, et al.

Verghese, Abraham
Cutting for Stone, et al.

~0~

In Memory

Sarah Cox 1926

"Steve" Stephenson 1925

Sarah Stigmon and Nancy Fanucchi 1982

Bob and Ivy Ross 1949

Made in the USA
Lexington, KY
06 October 2018